TRANSFORMATIONAL
LEADERSHIP

TRANSFORMATIONAL LEADERSHIP

* LOT'S OF PEOPLE TALK ABOUT IT, NOT MANY PEOPLE LIVE IT. IT'S NOT SEXY, SOFT, OR EASY.

Joshua Medcalf & Jamie Gilbert

ISBN: 1537096060
ISBN 13: 9781537096063

TABLE OF CONTENTS

CHAPTER 1

YOU MATTER

YOU DON'T NEED to spend too much time around me before I bring up Judah Smith. In my opinion he is the best in the world at sharing stories in public speaking, hands down.

Another one of my friends who does a lot of public speaking and is world renowned at his craft said, "Judah is the best, and no one else is even close."

I agree.

I've only spent about 5 minutes with Judah in a private setting and I chose my questions carefully. The first question I asked him was, "What do you know now that you wish you would have known when you first started out?"

Every week I study Judah's work. I listen to his mp3's. I've read his books. I listen to him speak live twice a week even though he gives the same talk twice, I take notes and stay for both. His thinking, writing, and speaking have *greatly* influenced all of mine. However, nothing has hit me as hard as his response to that question.

He said, "When I started out, I tried to write the BEST sermons. Now I just try and love the people in the audience."

When I started out, I tried to be the best in the world at performance psychology. My focus was teaching mental training exercises, tips, and tricks to increase performance.

Today, I start almost every talk with "YOU Matter."

I let people know that they matter.
Not what they do.
Not what they achieve.
Not their goals.
Not their stuff.
Not their accomplishments.
Not their dreams.
THEY matter.
YOU matter.
You are a human BEING, not just a human DOING.

I probably would have laughed at someone if they had tried to explain this to me 5 years ago. Now it is the most important part of what we do at Train To Be CLUTCH. We used to focus on performance enhancement, now we focus on helping people know and feel that they are loved unconditionally for who they ARE, not what they DO. Performance is secondary.

What you learn in this book, if applied consistently and carefully over time, can help you tap into your greatest potential as a person who leads people. BUT until you experience a true heart posture shift and value human beings for who they are, you will remain trapped in transactional leadership.

People can feel and know in their heart whether you really care about them, or if it is just a strategy. *It can't just be a strategy.*

I can't trust you to love me if you don't love yourself.
We can't give something we don't have.
We have to accept unconditional love before we can give it.

The challenge I've seen is that many people in leadership had parental figures who showed love sparingly, and the parents only showed up and gave love, attention, and affection when they *ACHIEVED* something.

This pattern created achievement addicts.
This pattern created approval addicts.

Underneath it all is a desperate need for approval and achievement, because deep down we think *that* is what makes us loveable. We think we aren't loveable without the doing and achieving.

But deep down we are all seeking authentic and deep unconditional love. We are tired of the performance.

Our HEART is tired.
Our SOUL is tired.

We can break the cycle.
You can break the cycle.

In order to break the cycle at a foundational level, you must understand that your value comes from who you are.

If you don't love yourself, how can you be trusted to love those you lead?

If you don't love yourself, you will always have a tendency to operate out of fear instead of love. (Believe me, I know from experience.)

Fear of losing love.
Fear of losing your job.
Fear of losing respect.
Fear of always having to prove something.

If you are looking to an outside source for worth, approval, and love, you will always operate out of the fear of losing it.

God already unconditionally loves you, and His steadfast love endures forever. It has never been about your performance, and it never will be about your performance. Therefore, you are free to accept His love, love yourself, and finally be freed to love others with no strings attached.

Who you become forever and always trumps what you achieve.

Transformational leadership has nothing to prove, only love to give.

"Perfect love casts out fear." (*English Standard Version*[1] 1 John 4:18)

We do not expect you to believe everything we believe, and even if you don't believe what we believe, we think you can find immense value from the stories, tools, and strategies within. Our hope is that you will feel encouraged, refreshed, and maybe even a little bit lighter after reading this book.

---

1 *The English Standard Version Bible*. New York: Oxford University Press, 2009. Print.

CHAPTER 2

TRANSFORMATIONAL VS. TRANSACTIONAL

MEMORIES OF TRANSACTIONAL leaders can haunt people for a lifetime.

Maybe it was a person who was your coach.
Maybe it was a person who was your pastor.
Maybe it was a person who was your teacher.
Maybe it was a person who was your boss.

Transactional leadership has a tell and a pattern. It usually makes people feel like production units.

I was sitting at a lunch with a lot of people who give money to support a certain BCS school's program when I heard the man responsible for leading the baseball program say, "Well, you have to remember that we have over 700 innings walking out the door next year." He was referring to the young men he had the responsibility of leading, but that little reference was a picture of his heart posture. They were production units first, not human beings.

"From the abundance of the heart the mouth speaks." (*ESV* Luke 6:34)

Many people tell me they felt more pressure from shooting or kicking a ball in little league, high school, or collegiate sports than they did later in life in what could be considered much more stressful situations.

In leadership:

What you say matters.
What you do matters.
HOW you do it matters even more.

Those things will likely be remembered for a lifetime by those you lead, and those leadership patterns also have a high likelihood of being passed down for generations.

You have a responsibility and opportunity to encourage, bring hope, and inspire. But too often this opportunity is soiled and the modus operandi in leadership is to take the easy way out and demean, criticize, and use people.

It is easy to get caught up in the moment and lose perspective. It is easy to believe that winning is what really matters, and it is SO EASY to justify.

If we don't win I can't provide for my family.
If I don't get this contract I will lose my job.
If I don't turn these numbers around I will be fired.

It's easy to find fault, criticize, and blame.
It's hard to take responsibility, have patience, and encourage.

Transformational leadership is the toughest, but most rewarding path you can embark on. It takes time and almost impossible patience. It is requires authentic vulnerability, linguistic intentionality, and a willingness to do the dirty work no one likes to do. It requires putting first things first, and people above profits and winning. Transformational leadership builds authentic relationships based on love, and helps build people into becoming everything they are capable of becoming.

Transformational leadership isn't soft; rather, it is a different kind of strength not easily recognized. It is the type of strength exhibited by people who can get struck in the cheek and have the courage not to fight back, even though they could. It is the strength of someone like Gandhi and MLK's non-violent resistance. It is the type of strength it takes for a kid in middle school to go over and sit with the person sitting by themselves at lunch.

Transactional leadership is shallow, sometimes quick, but lacks the depth of foundation needed to transform lives. It puts profits and winning above relationships, and it leaves a wake of emotional baggage and broken hearts. Transactional leaders push people toward performance-based identity prisons and the emotional roller coaster of finding your self-worth in achievement. *Transactional leadership builds relationships to find trigger points to manipulate people to get results.*

For many years I operated as a transactional leader, and I left a lot of hurting people in my wake.

The good news is that it is never too late to invest in yourself and make changes. Believing we can change is more than half the battle. If you want to become a transformational leader, you have to become a better you.

None of us were born leaders, and all of us slip up at times, myself probably more than Jamie. We have the privilege of mentoring and speaking into the lives of people all over the world from many different backgrounds and passions. Some of them are world class at what they do, and others are just beginning their journey. The thing that is consistent is that we get to see people learn, grow, and change for the better every single day.

The truth is, everyone is a mentor; it just takes some people longer to realize their role than others. I love what Joe Ehrmann says about mentorship in his book, *Inside Out Coaching*:

"Imagine if coaches (leaders) today thought of themselves as mentors or aspired to the ideals of mentoring: I am the head mentor or I'm the mentor of the defensive line. Think how much that might have changed the coach-player relationship—a title conveying an *UNDENIABLE OBLIGATION* to care for players' welfare, instruct them in virtue, and guide them toward an adulthood of citizenship and contemplation."

When I speak I operate under the assumption that at least one or two of the people in the room are actively considering taking their own life. We know a guy who coaches that had a person who played for him take her own life, and it changed his perspective on leadership forever. I want to lead and mentor as if hearts and lives are on the line, because I believe they truly are.

Would you operate differently if someone you were responsible for leading took their own life? Really think about that. Would winning or profits seem so important if that happened? *Too often manipulation is being disguised, rationalized, and justified as love, but those we lead aren't fooled and this only exasperates their pain.*

Too often I meet adults who still have scars that have never healed from transactional leadership that hurt and used them. You have probably had a similar experience with someone in leadership at some point in your life as well. It is disgusting and disdainful. Sometimes those people have done awful things and abused their power physically, but other times people in leadership have done significant damage emotionally without ever inappropriately touching a person.

Our world needs an influx of people committed to transformational leadership. We are honored and grateful for the opportunity to shed some light on how to become a transformational leader.

Becoming transformational is not practical, it's not easy, but it is transformational.

Please remember, most books like this are people writing advice to themselves, and this book is no exception ☺

CHAPTER 3

A SIMPLE PHRASE THAT GOT A GUY THROUGH NAVY SEAL "HELL WEEK"

THERE ARE SOME things in life that we don't *feel* like doing, but that we know are really beneficial for us. I think it's all those small things that really make a massive difference.

I was listening to a guy who served as a Navy SEAL speak to a group of young people in college and I can't forget what he said about something so small.

He went about his preparation for SEALs training differently than most people do. Most people enlist and go into training right out of high school, but he had just finished college and was at a different stage in life.

He knew he wanted to go into the Navy and before he enrolled he did his homework. He read everything he could on the SEALs and even interviewed a few former SEALs members and asked them about what they learned and what they would do differently. Talk about *real* hustle!

One of the things he knew was that the greatest period of fall out during the 2.5 years of becoming a Navy SEAL member was the 5-day period called "Hell Week". During that time, they would cover over 100 miles, do up to 20 hours of physical activity every day, and were only guaranteed 4 hours of sleep for the whole week.

Most of their running was done while carrying boats on top of their heads while they were dripping in frigid ocean water, beyond exhausted, with sand in every crevice, and with their superiors yelling at them to **ring the bell!** (Ringing the bell signifies a person quitting the Navy SEAL training program)

He smirked as he talked about a bald spot that carrying those boats created on his head.

From his preparation, he learned about something small. Something that most overlooked. What was it? Make sure you eat.

During the small breaks in their training they had meals provided to them. Now, you can imagine that if you were given 15 minutes after having only 2 hours of sleep in 2 days and having done close to 40 hours of physical practice, you would take the opportunity to sleep. It makes complete sense. But many of the guys would be so overtired and exhausted that they actually chose not to eat.

I've been through some tough workouts, probably not to the level of their training, but I know how hard it is to eat immediately after a workout. It's the last thing you want to do.

But this guy knew what was most important. He knew that the training was so hard that he could not operate on an empty stomach and the lack of eating was one of the biggest reasons for people not completing the training.

Knowing this, during his downtime, all he would say to himself was "Calories, calories, calories."

Yes, closing his eyes was VERY appealing. In fact, it would even be helpful. Many believed it was the *most* pressing issue. But he knew that if he really wanted to thrive in his training, he had to focus on the *most important* little thing in that moment.

We must become aware of differentiating the *most important* from the *most pressing.*

I hear it again and again from everyone. Whether it's the nine year-old I train, people in professional sports, people who lead businesses, parents, people coaching in college or people playing in college:

"I don't have enough time to read."

Like the cleverly titled book *Too Busy NOT To Pray,* there is too much on the line not to read. Not having time to read is like saying you don't have time to eat or exercise. If you don't fuel your heart with what it needs, you CANNOT operate anywhere near your potential.

Personally, I read a lot, but rarely do I get excited about sitting down to read. Every now and then I will feel like it, but mostly, I can think of many other things that I *want* to do in the moment.

Sometimes I am tired and drained. Other times I just want to go to bed and nap like my two year old.

But when I approach a book now I say to myself *"Calories, calories, calories!"* I have found this is better to say in my head than out loud most of the time ☺

Remember......

- You don't have to read.
- You don't have to do a cue card.
- You don't have to do a What Went Well journal.

- You don't have to train your facial expression.
- You don't have to create autonomy in your group.
- You don't have to ask growth mindset questions.
- You don't *have to* do anything.

But what I know is that **for everyone of us, there is a gap between who we are and who we want to become. There is a gap between where we are and where we want to be. What helps us close those gaps are the small things that we *consistently* choose to commit to over and over and over.**

They may seem insignificant while you are doing them, but like the meals in the middle of Hell Week, they are *essential* to our pursuit in becoming a transformational leader.

I don't know how long you will need to do them to get to a point where they are second nature. I don't know which ones are going to be the most important for you and your particular context and make-up. But I do know that there is no growth without committing to the small stuff.

Moving toward our greatest potential never *feels* great, but it always affects change. It's most often dirty hard work. It comes from things that are done well when no one is around and no one is watching.

The bright lights are coming, but they only reveal our work in the dark.

The storms will come. If you haven't prepared for them, if you haven't built a solid foundation, *you will* get swept away.

Are you ready to start building?

It all starts with trust.....

TRUST? IN WHO??

REGARDLESS OF YOUR personal thoughts on Jesus I hope we can agree on
two things about Him:

1.) His life split time, as we know it. As in BC/AD.
2.) Twelve of His thirteen followers and the person who wrote 2/3
of the New Testament were willing to be beaten, tortured, crucified, and killed for what they believed was the Truth: that Jesus
lived, was crucified, resurrected and that He appeared to them
numerous times after His resurrection.

For us, Jesus is the perfect model of transformational leadership. In less
than three years He inspired a movement that is still growing today, and
millions of people have literally been willing to give their lives for that
Truth.

If you want to look at the historical evidence for Jesus' life, we suggest reading the book, *More Than A Carpenter*, which details the incredible historical accuracy of His life, death, and resurrection. Joshua
McDowell was an atheist who set out to prove the Bible was a myth, and
through his research he found just the opposite. Historically speaking,
no other event in ancient history has better historical evidence than the
Bible.

So, for us, transformational leadership starts with trusting Jesus with
your life. The storms are coming, and we hope you will have something

greater than your performance to rely upon. I know for me, I have failed, I am going to fail at leadership, and rather than trust in my performance, I would rather trust in His performance.

CHAPTER 5

THE STORMS WILL COME

WHEN THE STORMS come, and they always come...

When life punches you in the face and bad things happen...

What will you do?

In whom or in what will you trust?

My brother Jonathan is very comfortable on a boat because he loves fishing and spends a lot of his free time on the water. I most likely couldn't even start our family boat; and certainly wouldn't want to navigate it through rough waters.

When the storms and rough waters come in your life, (and they always come) who do you want to have in your boat?

The disciples of Jesus were professional fishermen before they became his disciples. They were accustomed to weather changes and sudden winds, which swept through the valley across the Sea of Galilee. One day, Jesus told the disciples to get in a boat and take him to another town. This was fairly routine for them and they did exactly as he asked. Although they were PRO FISHERMEN, they encountered a storm that they believed was going to kill them. Curiously, in the middle of all this chaos Jesus was sleeping.

How could Jesus have been sleeping in the bottom of the boat when his disciples felt like they were going to die? And not only was He sleeping, but one of the accounts details that He was sleeping well on a little pillow.

When the disciples found him sleeping they were angry! "Jesus, how can you be asleep, don't you care that WE all are going to die?!" Notice, they included Jesus in that group.

The disciples were like many of us: we have had a hard time trusting Jesus when we go through the inevitable storms of life.

Think about this though... It was even harder when a storm came and *the disciples were going exactly where HE ASKED them to go.*

Have you ever felt like Jesus has fallen asleep in your boat?
Have you ever felt like He isn't in control, or that He doesn't care?

The disciples thought Jesus didn't care, because in their minds as fishermen, they had a picture of what it looked like when you cared. Maybe it was helping throw water back overboard. Maybe it was shouting encouragement to them. Maybe it was giving them a hug and telling them He loved them.

Whatever it was, Jesus was not fulfilling *their expectations.*

Our past experiences often hinder our ability to trust Jesus. Where was Jesus when my two year-old brother drowned? And where was He when my dad's cancer wasn't healed? If God really cared, would He have let them die? Would He let bad things happen to me?

I'm sure you have plenty of your own questions as well.

What I have come to realize is that Jesus is *always* in the boat with us, and He is able to sleep through the storm because He has it all under control. It never feels like He is in control when the waves are crashing over the sides of the boat, but He is, and that is why He can sleep like a baby.

In the disciples' situation, Jesus eventually went to the upper part of the boat and He calmed the storm. The disciples were in awe that the wind and waves obeyed Him. Maybe Jesus didn't handle it as quickly as *they* would have liked Him to, but He did and **does** have everything under control.

We GET to make choices, and our choices have pro-sequences and con-sequences, but ultimately God is in control. We have choices because if we didn't have a choice, then that would not be love, and God is perfect love.

> Proverbs 3:5-6 says: Trust in the Lord with all your heart and do not lean on your own understanding, in all your ways acknowledge Him, and He will direct your paths. (*New International Version*[2] Proverbs 3:5-6)

It sounds simple, and it is, but it's not easy. It is definitely counter-cultural for those who live in the United States where we largely believe in pulling ourselves up by the bootstraps. Trusting God takes faith and we don't always understand how, but ultimately He does direct our paths.

Maybe I'm crazy, but I don't have enough faith to believe we got here by accident or from a Big Bang. Everywhere I look around the world I see things that have been created: televisions, this computer I am typing on, my golf bag, backpack, shoes, books, my bed, my clothes, they all

---

2 *Holy Bible: New International Version*. (2011). Grand Rapids, Mich.: Zondervan.

have an intelligent designer. *I just don't have enough faith to believe the most intelligent beings on the planet weren't created by an intelligent designer.*

Those same disciples, minus Judas who betrayed Jesus and then killed himself, all followed Jesus and believed He was God until He was crucified. At that point, because they were fearful, they all abandoned Him, and hid. Jesus' most adamant and oldest disciple, Peter, had told Jesus three times the night before, "There is NO WAY I would ever deny you!" Then he went on to deny Jesus to a middle school girl three times less than 24 hours after making that bold claim to Jesus about never denying Him.

When Jesus died, all the disciples abandoned Him. Was God sleeping? Did He care? He wasn't sleeping and He did care and He allowed His only Son to die and rise again so that we would have eternal life. How did the disciples have the courage to preach that Jesus was the Son of God all over the known world, not fearing punishment and ultimately their death, without ever denying Him again? I believe the only thing that could have caused that drastic change was that they actually saw Jesus and spent time with Him after He was resurrected. It was easy to entrust their lives to a risen Jesus.

Maybe you haven't *seen* Jesus. We certainly haven't either. But His presence is real in this world. There is no greater way to be in his presence than to read some of the Scriptures for yourself. If you want ideas on where to begin or would like to speak with us about that, please reach out. Our contact info is at the end of the book.

So many people in leadership, including ourselves, have tried to find security in our performances. At times it feels good, safe, and secure. *But when the storms come in life, will that title, trophy, bank statement, or position really be what you hold onto?*

It's simple, I choose to trust Him and His performance, rather than my own. I hope you do too because no one on earth has ever been offered a better deal than the one that Jesus freely offers you and me. All it takes is faith and trust.

"He has been a great God to me—my rock and my support. When I would get cut from a team or told I wasn't good enough, God never cut me. He never said I wasn't good enough. Personally, I am on a crusade to lift Him up in everything I do. People have to see Christ in us, and I am trying to emphasize that with all of the people I meet.

–Kevin Ollie after winning the 2014 Men's Basketball NCAA Championship

CHAPTER 6

MESSAGE IN A BOTTLE

WE GET SENT a lot of stories from people who have read our work or have used the tools we have given them, but this story really stood out to me. Kate sent it to us after having read the PDF version of this book about the chapter immediately before this one, so I asked Kate if we could share it. She said we could, so here it is.....

"August 1st of this summer, I went into the ER after a routine shoulder surgery because I wasn't feeling well. I couldn't put my finger on what was wrong. I just knew something was not quite right.

On a hunch they checked some blood work and did a CT scan of my lungs, where they found a big fat blood clot lodged in there. My grandmother died of a Pulmonary Embolism, it's the one thing I told the surgeon I was terrified of, and there I was staring it in the face.

They gave me a newer drug to treat it and admitted me a few days to stabilize me and then sent me home.

Again I felt like something wasn't right, I begged the doctor to let me stay one more day, but they insisted all was well and sent me home.

Within hours of being home I fell asleep and then woke up suddenly and couldn't control my speech or my muscles. I was having a severe reaction to the blood-thinning drug they gave me. In front of my 3 kids, I looked like I was having a full-fledged stroke and was taken out the front door to an ambulance.

I was admitted for another week and a half, which fell during my kids first week of school that I have never missed. They tried other drugs while I was there and talked about **the high risk of having a stroke or another embolism that could kill me instantly.**

I had nurses give me the wrong medicine or accidently double dose pills, mistakes everywhere, doctors all with different opinions, constant signatures on forms about how dangerous each drug was before they could give it to me, and I was relentlessly filled with paralyzing fear that no one was in control, that I was alone. I'd never felt so deserted, and I sat in my hospital bed hugging my pillow and praying and asking God why he had forgotten about me.

As I sat there looking ahead and feeling like my life will never be normal anymore, my husband walked in to visit, and asked me if I wanted anything. I hadn't been eating and all I really wanted was some caffeine to get rid of a headache so I asked him to sneak me a diet coke from the vending machine down the hall. As he left to get me a coke I sat in my bed, numb and fully alone. He got back to the room and he just looked at me and said, you're not going to believe this...

He hands me the coke and on the back, it has my name. **Kate.** *I know that Coke had that ridiculous marketing campaign where they put names on all the Coke bottles but I'd never seen one with my name on it - despite having a common name, and bored in grocery store lines, I always looked.*

But really what are the chances that in a machine outside my hospital room, a random coke bottle was going to come out with my name on it right at the time that I was begging for God to tell me he hadn't forgotten about me.

I still have that bottle, it's in my kitchen on the windowsill, reminding me to be thankful and never doubt that He is with me, even when I don't think I see Him there. It's kind of a strange thing to think a coke bottle sent me a message but I have no doubt that was no coincidence. :)"

CHAPTER 7

SOME PEOPLE WEAR "BUSYNESS" LIKE A BADGE OF HONOR

SOME PEOPLE WEAR "busyness" like a badge of honor.

I hear people say, "it must be nice to have time to read, but I'm too busy for that."

It's always said in a way that I hear "It must be nice to have time to read, but I'm out feeding starving children in Africa, building water wells in third world countries, and building schools for kids who just want an education."

And if you are Adam Braun or Scott Harrison, who created two of my favorite mission driven organizations that do those things, then by all means I apologize for *MAKING* time to read.

But the sad reality is for most people, you're not doing those things.

It's like we completely lost sight at some point that we have volition. That we are the humanoid, flesh and blood, that has the greatest say about our life.

You CHOOSE your schedule every day.

You CHOOSE what you will ignore every day.

You CHOOSE what you will give your time to every day.

The bottom line is that we make time and give our time to what we value. The problem is some of us value being busy. It makes us feel good; studies have even shown it releases dopamine in our brains.[3]

The HARD thing to do is not allow yourself to become infected with the disease of busyness and actually spend your time doing the work and spending your time on the things that matter most.

Last time I checked, who you become is pretty high on that list.

*The only resource that is the exact same for everyone in the world is **time**, and depending on how you use what you have today will impact how much or how little you have of it in the future.*

Let's stop glorifying busyness.

Let's start putting first things first.

Who and what gets your best energy every day?

Don't just skim over that...WHO and WHAT gets your best energy everyday?

You can always make more money, but you can never get more time.

Time is the most valuable resource in the world. Are you investing it or wasting it?

---

3 http://m.psychologytoday.com/blog/brain-wise/201209/why-were-all-addicted-texts-twitter-and-google

"But I have a mortgage and a job!!"

Well, maybe you could benefit from making some temporary sacrifices (investments) for who you want to become.

Maybe you could move back into your parents' basement to free up resources and time to read and experiment with your passion.

Maybe it's time to stop treating what you do like a hobby and start becoming deliberate about beating on your craft.

Maybe it's time to do a time inventory and see where you ACTUALLY spend your time every week.

Maybe it's time to tell your boss no and your family yes.

Maybe it's time to build a better system so you stop having to waste time manually doing things that can be automated.

Maybe it's time to start delegating responsibility to those who are waiting for you to trust them.

Maybe it's time to tell the coffee, sugar, and meat, NO, and your overall energy level, YES.

Maybe it's time to give your family less material things and more of your love and energy.

Maybe it's time to start saying NO to instant gratification and YES to investing in yourself.

Take an honest assessment of how you spend your time and see how much of it falls under what, Sogyal Rinpoche, calls "active laziness":

using our time on tasks that make us feel responsible, but that might be more appropriately labeled, "irresponsibilities."[4]

It's time we stop wearing busyness as a badge of honor and glorifying it as something to be proud of and start making the tough choices to put first things first and make sure our best energy is going into the people and work that matters most.

It's impossible to become transformational if you insist on continually being too busy. Seasons of your life will be busier than others, but if busyness isn't just a season and it is a way of life, then it is time to make some serious changes.

TRAIN TO BE CLUTCH

- Keep track of how you use your time for the next 3 days in 15-minute increments. Determine whether or not how you use your time upholds or negates your values, principles, and commitments.

---

4 Diana Kaplan's article on busyness https://medium.com/thelist/the-cult-of-

CHAPTER 8

MISSION DRIVEN > GOAL DRIVEN

SINCE PUBLISHING OUR first book, Burn Your Goals, people often ask us "Do you REALLY mean you shouldn't have goals?" Or "What is the difference between a goal and a mission?"

The answer to the first question is, YES, we really mean we think you shouldn't have goals.

Secondly, we think the difference between goal driven and mission driven is MASSIVE!

I think Jamie sums it up very succinctly when he tells people, goals are something you achieve; a dream or mission is who you become.

Let's look at Mother Theresa's life as an example. Mother Theresa is one of the greatest examples of a mission driven life and transformational leadership.

What was her mission? *To serve the needs of the sick and the dying.*

That's it.

Oh, and her most common advice to people: *start with one, and you don't need to go across the world, your backyard will do just fine.*

I think most people like **BIG AUDACIOUS** goals because they are sexy. It's not sexy to start in your backyard or start with one. It's not sexy to start selling individual matches door to door. It's not sexy to build something in your parents' garage or in your dorm room.

A mission is something you can do today, right where you are, using what you have, and you don't need anyone's permission.

A goal is just the opposite. You need permission to be a doctor, a lawyer, an NBA General Manager, or a CEO of a Fortune 500 company. And goals often have the opposite effect from Mother Theresa's advice: they cause us to look right past the one in our own backyard.

Transformational leadership is all about being ridiculously faithful with the one in your own backyard. If we do that for long enough, we might just wake up one day to realize our back yard of influence is now the entire world.

"The questions that will matter most on your deathbed are the questions related to your relationships. What kind of husband was I? What kind of wife? What kind of partner? What kind of father? What kind of son? What kind of daughter? What kind of member of the community? What kind of coach? Who did I love and who loved me?" –Joe Ehrmann

CHAPTER 9

MORE THAN A MISSION STATEMENT

HE WAS SO excited telling me about their sports program and how different they were from everyone else. I was just asking questions and trying to learn as we headed from the airport to the venue I would be speaking at that evening.

The audience would be around a thousand people and I wanted to learn as much as I could in case something important needed to be addressed.

He had to have mentioned the word "mission" at least three or four times when talking about what separated their program from others in the region. So naturally I ended up asking, "What is your programs' mission?"

Silence....

.....

.....

"Well.......

It's......

Something about...."

He pulls out his phone and starts looking it up I assumed.

Trying to be polite I asked a different question and spared him some time while he was looking.

This experience is far from an anomaly, and in our experience it is sadly the norm.

Observed in isolation it is not that big of deal.

The issue is a collective experience compounded over time.

To me it reminds me of the videos that have been popping up on my Facebook feed lately with people wearing secret cameras while walking around New York City.

One of the videos is a woman who just walks around the city and you hear all the "cat calls" and approaches she ignored over the 10 hours of walking.

The other video was of a man, who claims to date members of the same sex, who is carrying around a Victoria Secret shopping bag in a feminine manner while walking around for a few hours.

Any of the incidents taken in isolation are not that big of a deal, and most people could probably psychologically shake them off, BUT taken collectively, and compounded over time you start to get a very scary picture of the emotional, psychological, and even potential physical damage this must cause.

We encountered a similar phenomenon when we called all 180 of the people who coach women's college golf and who were attending the National Convention we were speaking at.

We asked three very simple questions to everyone who answered or called us back.

1.) What is your mission in coaching?
2.) What is your mission for your program?
3.) How can we serve you?

It was highly alarming hearing their answers, or lack there of, to the first two questions.

Often "winning championships" was one of the first things out of their mouth, and other times the question was met with "I'm not really sure" or "I haven't really thought about that."

Ironically, one notable exception was a woman named Andrea Gaston. Her mission had nothing to do with golf, and it had a lot to do with serving her young women and helping them develop as people. Andrea has also won three national championships at USC.

If you don't know your mission in the comfortable confines of car on the way to an event, good luck having it guide you when you are facing the tough decisions that you will face in your life of leadership.

Often times we don't get time to think about how we want to act, or what we want to do, we have to make a split-second decision. *If your mission hasn't been well thought out and deeply impressed upon your heart than it is not guiding your life.*

Your mission needs to be so important to you and everyone you lead that it is immediately available when asked for it. There should be no hesitation, because of how engrained and rehearsed the mission is in your daily lives.

It's more than a cool mission statement on your website or a design that hangs on your wall. It's the principles that guide you every-day in both the most simple of tasks, as well as in the most trying of circumstances.

Our mission is:

Transformed hearts. Transformed minds. Through love and mentorship.

Love people. Serve people. Provide value.

To become love, so everywhere we go people will want what we have.

What is your mission?

TRAIN TO BE CLUTCH

- Joe Ehrman said, "We are successful when we give something our all," and to that I would add, are we giving our all to the things that matter most in life?
- What do you want to be remembered for when you are faced with death?
- Everyone in your life needs to know your mission and they, and you, need to hear about the mission as often as possible.
- Ask others what their mission statement is and copy it, steal it, alter it, until you find something that is deeply meaningful to you.
- Most importantly, how are you intentionally living out that mission today?

"Think what would happen if coaches chose to use their position to build and repair their players' hearts and minds. Imagine if every player understood that he or she had a personal responsibility to contribute to the betterment of society by identifying his or her unique cause." –Joe Erhmann

CHAPTER 10

A NEW WAY TO OPERATE

ABOUT TWO YEARS ago my life drastically changed when I started each morning with gratefulness prayer and meditation in the shower.

It is so easy to get swept up in all the seemingly urgent things that require our attention, but I have found my days go much better now that I've made gratefulness prayer a non-negotiable in my daily life.

There are three reasons I do mine in the shower. The first is habit stacking, as my friend James Clear calls it. I know I'm going to take a shower before I start my day at least 300 days out of the year, and no matter where I'm at in the world, I know there is a really good chance I'm going to shower. So, I stacked gratefulness prayer on top of another habit that was already very ingrained in my life. Habit stacking like this increases my likelihood of sticking to it.

The other two reasons are simple: I like to take long showers and the shower is a place where our brain waves slow down making meditation much easier.

Operating out of gratefulness rather than constantly being pulled up and down by results is a much healthier way for me to operate. I still find myself getting pulled by results, but not nearly as much after incorporating this exercise.

With our team at UCLA we do an exercise before practice every day called, One Breath One Mind, which is an exercise Phil Jackson had his teams do for similar purposes. We all hold hands in a circle and take deep breaths in and out while focusing on one word for the day. One person counts out the seconds so we know how long to breathe in and to sync up our breathing. We do this exercise for about two minutes.

No matter what you do to facilitate operating from a place of unconditional gratitude, it is one of the most powerful things you can do.

I've found that starting my day thanking God for all the things in my life, including clean drinking water and all the doors that have closed in my life, allows me to operate with more peace, greater clarity, and a healthier perspective.

Simply put, operating from a place of unconditional gratitude gives me a greater likelihood of having more transformational encounters with those I lead.

TRAIN TO BE CLUTCH

Download the book "Transform Your Habits" for free at jamesclear. com/habits

THE LEARNING ZONE = THE UNCOMFORTABLE ZONE

"BUT THIS IS so uncomfortable."

I often hear these words regarding our training when working with people who play sports. I smile and respond with the following:

*"Of course it is, that is **The Point**. Our growth is severely restricted when we only operate within our comfort zone. I would not be helping you if I didn't push you to failure."*

The wisest teachers know the difference between the comfort zone, the learning zone and the panic zone.

The comfort zone is a great place to live on Sunday afternoons, eating cheese dip, watching NFL football and checking on your fantasy football team. But, if you want to change yourself and the world, then you must resist the temptation to live in the comfort zone.

The learning zone lies just outside of the exterior wall of the comfort zone. In this zone, we fail, we struggle, and we often become frustrated. Many people want to quit during this transition; however, transformational leadership is about coming alongside the developing person, encouraging the failure, offering immediate feedback and support, and naming this part of the journey as THE path to growth and mastery.

The Panic zone lies beyond the learning zone and is too far outside of the comfort zone. Inviting an athlete to operate in this realm can do more harm because the new task is too much of a stretch and far exceeds his/her physical and mental capabilities. I have seen tears, tantrums and breakdowns result from people coaching and parenting pushing others into the panic zone.

There is a path and process to growth. A person who is highly skilled at teaching basketball doesn't begin to teach the proper mechanics of a jump shot from the three-point line. No, they begin close to the basket and teach the importance of proper foot placement, balance, hand placement on the ball... Parents of babies do not force their child to walk before they learn how to crawl. The baby must master the physical, visual and cognitive tasks of crawling before they can learn to walk.

Learning to be comfortable being uncomfortable is a skill that can and should be developed.

*The more we are sensitized to uncomfortable feelings the more we realize they are temporary, and with additional practice, repetitions and persistence, the outer edge of the comfort zone expands. Fear of failure, fear of the unknown and fear of the uncomfortable dramatically **decreases** the more we experience them.*

Once we master a new skill, we often forget the trials, tribulations and hours of failure it took to learn the skill. Therefore, people who are transformational leaders invite others to reflect upon the journey in order to remember the historic struggles to master a task, which was once the learning zone that has now become their new comfort zone. This recognizing and remembering helps to solidify the process-oriented reality of growth.

Living in the learning zone invites more adventures and requires more attention to our own growth in transformational leadership.

TRAIN TO BE CLUTCH

- How can you model this process for those you lead?
- Where can you push the outer edges of your comfort zone, embracing failure in order to share your humanity and encourage the growth of those in your sphere of influence?

TOUCH THE NEEDLE

I'LL NEVER FORGET the day I walked in to work with a horrendous cold. I used to work in a health foods shop for a lady from China who also owned an eastern medical clinic with certified acupuncture therapists. I had never been before, but when I came in to work with a horrible cold, she insisted I go see the lady for acupuncture.

I don't know if my experience was normal, but this is what happened. They had me lie down on a bed and they proceeded to strategically place needles all over my body.

Then the therapists left the room. After a few minutes of me lying there listening to the sounds of the sea CD, a lady returned. She gently went to each needle and did something so simple, yet so effective. She touched the top of it, and boom! Like a floodgate bursting open I felt heat or energy exuding from each needle and swelling throughout my body.

She then left the room for another period of time. She returned to touch the needles a few more times resulting in the same sensations.

The feeling was amazing! But I thought the *process* was even more astounding.

She put the needles in place. And once in place, all that was required was she simply touch the top.

When I observe many of the people I get to work with who coach, lead, and parent, most run around like a doctor in an emergency room moving up and down the body frantically tying this, injecting that, connecting these tubes and asking questions incessantly.

I won't say it's not effective. But what is *effective* is not always **equipping**. If there is one word that rests at the heart of transformational leadership, it is equipping.

When I help people who are trying to move toward becoming transformational in their leadership, I think of the acupuncture therapist. I try to help them set the needles by creating healthy boundaries and controllable expectations, and then give them the encouragement to touch the needle by enforcing those healthy boundaries.

- **Set the standards and values.**
- **Equip the people you lead with tools to self-regulate.**
- **Touch the needle by asking simple questions, giving short pieces of guidance, and by enforcing the healthy boundaries.**

CHAPTER 13

CAUSE THEM TO LEARN

WHEN YOU HEAR the word teach, what ideas or images come to mind?

Is it a person who teaches with a pointer and an old-school chalkboard drilling information into your mind?

Is it a person who coaches drawing on a whiteboard moving the magnets and dissecting plays?

Is it your parents holding a shoe with you draped over their laps saying "I will teach you a lesson!!"?

Or is it a person pastoring a church sharing a sermon on stage behind a pulpit?

I remember a guy who taught at the, *Irish Bible Institute*, saying something about teaching that rocked my world, and hopefully it does yours.

We were looking at Deuteronomy where it says:

"You shall love the Lord your God with all your heart and with all your soul and with all your might. And these words I have commanded you today shall be on your heart. You shall **TEACH** them diligently to your children…?" (*ESV* Deut 6:5-6)

He put his bible down and said, "The Hebrew word for *teach* actually means **To Cause To Learn**."

Suspenseful? Not really.
Paradigm altering? Perhaps.

As I get to travel and spend time with people who educate, lead, parent and coach in various fields, levels, and contexts I am astounded at how many of them, myself included, practice teaching as though it's as simple as dispensing information.

It's like giving our children their medicine. We put it on a spoon. They open their mouths. And now they have it. Done.

"I told you before, this is how you come off of the screen!"

"We just talked about that in the scouting report!"

"How many times do I have to tell you that the report has to be in *this* format!?"

"I told you that your toys have to be put away in those drawers over there!"

Sound familiar?

Just because I dispense information does not mean someone has learned it. They have to choose to soak it in. And we play a vital role in that interaction.

Phil Jackson said, "The most we can hope for is to create the best possible conditions for success, then let go of the outcomes."

How do we shift toward creating this environment?

1. Heart Posture of Love and Care

I have learned that in teaching and public speaking, people remember less of what I said, and more about how I made them feel. I honestly believe that I subconsciously feel someone's heart posture toward me before they ever say a word to me. Maybe it has to do with their physical posture, facial expression, or how they carry themselves, but most often I get a sense almost immediately as to whether or not this person really cares for me.

And I am not talking about having each person you lead sit in your office and share their life details. We don't have to have Dr. Phil sessions with each of the people we lead. I know far too many people in leadership who want the details of people's lives and then end up *using* them to manipulate and control that person.

Caring for people is taking a genuine interest in *their* interests and well being without any ulterior motive. They need to feel your heart posture saying, "I love you, regardless of what you do. I care about your hopes and dreams. I care about YOU, not just what you do. I want to help you become everything you are capable of being."

Gregg Popovich said, "If a player knows that you really care and can make him better, you got a guy for life."

Our heart posture changes as we suspend our judgments on others. I work ridiculously hard on separating who someone is from what they do or have done. I try to treat them with unconditional love. I am nowhere near perfect at it, but the more I work on accepting God's unconditional love for me, the more I treat people with that same love.

Wanted: Encouragers
The world has enough critics already.

2. Create an Environment Where Questions Are Valued

One of the top attributes of teams and individuals who I believe are thriving is their ability and resolve to ask questions.

Sadly in our society, we are afraid of seeming like we don't have it altogether or that we didn't get it the first time so we don't speak up. Many of us operate with a fixed mindset where our mistakes define us. So no one wants to mess up or seem like they don't understand something. But wouldn't you know it, when one person asks a question, most people agree that they don't quite get it either.

I remember in grade school where reading textbooks out loud was the norm. I raised my hand to read and proceeded down the page until I made a big mistake. A HUGE one! Instead of pronouncing the word "organism" I boldly said "orgasm." I have no idea where that came from, but Mrs. B flipped! And thus ended my career of volunteering to read publicly.

I met a few people recently and one of the guys said something, and everyone else started laughing. So I joined in, not wanting to be the weirdo. Then he said, "Have you seen that movie?" BUSTED! I hadn't seen the movie and I didn't even know what he said. I just didn't want to stand out for not *getting it!* If only I would have been comfortable asking the question, "I didn't get it. What did you say?"

Yes the question might be basic and the answer may be something obvious, but if we create a culture where there is no such thing as a stupid question, we foster an environment where learning and failing are encouraged. Simply put, we push people toward a growth mindset.

3. Suspend the Parameters of Time

I think that more pain, anxiety, and frustration come from trying to make people "get it" in a short period of time.

- Of course we'd want our spouse to reach out to a fantastic friend of ours about having a mentoring relationship.
- Of course I wish I would have understood the growth mindset two years ago the way I do now.
- Of course we want our kids to utilize the unfathomable resources at their disposal.
- Of course we want our colleagues to learn to hustle the way that we do.
- Of course we want our team to flawlessly know the offense and defensive schemes by the start of the season.

But, the harder we try to squeeze water in our hands, the less of it we end up with. The harder we try to push people to learn, the more anxiety they tend to have about learning. We must create an environment for learning; and getting frustrated and yelling rarely accomplish this.

In my experience, helping people come to "Aha" moments is more of an art than a science, though there certainly is science involved. But I whole-heartedly stand by what Adam Braun encourages:

"You can't inject someone with education the way you can with a vaccine. You can't force it upon people. They have to reach out and work for it themselves."
~ Adam Braun, *The Promise Of A Pencil*

TRAIN TO BE CLUTCH
Today, work on creating an environment ripe for transformation by:

- Focusing on treating those you lead according to *who they are*, not what they have done.

44

- Try this exercise: Write out your team members' names down with a blank space beside each.
- Jessica is _____.
- First in regards to how you feel according to what they have done.
    - Jessica is <u>Lazy and all she does is complain.</u>
    - John is <u>a pain in the butt!</u>
  - Secondly according to who they are.
    - Jessica is <u>A person created in God's image and a good communicator</u>
    - John is <u>a child of God and he has the potential to be resilient under pressure.</u>

- Encourage questions and say, "That's a great question! I love your eagerness to learn!"
- Let go of the need to have change NOW! Focus on sowing seeds.
- Regularly read 10 minutes of *How To Stop The Pain* by James Richards.

"First, as I have said repeatedly, coaches have an unparalleled platform, power, and position with which to model, teach, and redefine masculinity and femininity."
–Joe Ehrmann

CHAPTER 14

IS THAT REALLY *YOUR* DREAM?

IF THERE IS one thing that drives me up the wall, it is someone I just met asking me "What do you do?"

I have come up with a myriad of responses to that question:

- "Are you asking what I do to make money and provide for my family?"
- "I do a lot of things. I like to write, sing, play golf, etc..."
- "I serve as a professional story teller."
- "I get to mentor people in all walks of life."
- "I am uncomfortable with that question."
- "The sky is blue." (Joshua's personal favorite.)

Inevitably there is 30-foot stretch of path at my home golf course between the 1st green and the 2nd tee where this question perpetually seems to be asked.

One day I was playing with a younger guy who plays competitive golf and we reached this stretch of path. Trying to redeem that ground, I asked what I think is a better question:

"Sam, what is your dream?"

Without hesitation, he replied, "I want to play on the PGA Tour!"

I took a few seconds, smiled at him, and then asked one of the best questions I've ever asked:

"Is that really *your* dream, or is that just how you define success in your sport?"

I get to ask people a lot of questions, and I have never seen someone so puzzled and dumbfounded. He tried to talk, but every time he opened his mouth he just paused and went deep into thought.

Maybe it was his dream, or maybe it was just the dream that was conditioned in his mind.

As I work with people across sport and business I am astounded at how many people *say* they want to operate at the highest level of their sport or industry, but later reveal that they truly want something else. It's as if there is shame in not wanting to play professionally.

If you do want to play at the highest level, great!
If you do want to operate at the highest level in your industry, wonderful!

But please don't do it because you think reaching that level is the only way you can be successful. Do it because it is *your* dream.

I am consistently asked what the difference is between a dream and a goal. Here's what we believe.

A dream is:

- Something deep in your heart that has been there since you were young.

- Something you would do even if you weren't getting paid for it.
- Something that has a purpose beyond yourself.

What is your dream? Write it down. Don't worry though, sometimes we can't fully articulate our dreams until we are living them.

Is that really *your* dream or is that simply how you define success in your profession, education, sport, or relationship?

CHAPTER 15

IT'S LIKE PULLING A 20-TON BUS

"Nothing is changing! I just keep reverting to my same old ways!" she said as she had another performance that was below average. She was angry. And she had every right to be.

I mean for 16 years she has talked to herself in the *least beneficial* way possible. For 16 years she had trained herself to replay her mistakes over and over again in her mind. For the majority of her life she has allowed herself to believe that her identity and value come from the results.

Of course she should be angry. Because she has been invested in our training for a grand total of 7 days!

Everything in our society leads us toward believing that change must happen now and it must be final. We want results now with the smallest bit of investment possible and once we begin in a new direction we think that there is no way we should ever struggle to move forward.

How many times have we seen someone in sports rush back from a knee surgery only to do more damage?

How many church plants and start-ups have we seen flop because they didn't take the time to develop real and genuine relationships?

How many of us have ever started a workout plan or diet only to see it last for a few days or weeks?

It's ridiculous. I tell people all of the time:

This is not a little pill that you take once and everything changes. We are not, "think and be clutch" "do this once and be clutch" or even "be clutch."
Our brand is *Train To Be Clutch*. We become the people we train to be.

If you ever watch ESPN late at night you might find one of those *filler* programs showing the World's Strongest Man competitions. I used to watch those when I was younger and I was always fascinated by one event.

One of these large men would put on a harness that was tied to a bus or semi-truck. The object was to pull the vehicle around 25 meters as fast as possible. It was amazing to watch these jacked men lean forward, dig their feet in, and struggle to the point of bursting just to get the bus moving the initial few inches. Starting is tough. That makes total sense.

Although it's crucial, it's not just the start that counts. Once the bus is in motion the most critical component the rest of the race is rhythm. If the person was controlled and smooth as they stepped forward there would be no jerking in the rope and the resistance would not increase. Though there was still resistance, there was less friction when they had a consistent rhythm.

The hardest part was watching someone who would get the vehicle moving, only to jerk at the rope. They would create slack in the rope and then the inevitable would happen: the bus would stop or slow down. And getting that initial momentum once more would be the near impossible challenge at hand.

This is how I see it with transformational leadership and mental training. Many people work extremely hard to get the bus moving. They dive into reading, being aware of self-talk, focusing on loving and encouraging those they lead, not using fitness as a punishment, focusing on what your team does well, being intentional about sowing good beliefs, finding a way to believe things are in their best interest, constructively visualizing, and doing their cue card and what went well journals.

But when the novelty wears off and they hit the inevitable plateau on the path to mastery, the consistency and intentionality begin to fade. They are tempted to revert to old habits and patterns because those they lead aren't responding quick enough.

"This is hard."
"They aren't responding."
"I don't feel like this is making a difference."
"I don't have enough time to do this today."

Sound familiar?

Here is the thing, we need to be deliberate and consistent. Joshua says all the time "Patience, persistence, and passion will help you succeed *even if* your strategy is poor."

It is easy to snap at people when they don't do what we want.

It is easy to focus on everything that needs to be better.

It is easy to blame.

It is easy to create a culture of fear and manipulation.

Transformation takes time and it is often a much slower process than we would like. It is always harder and takes longer than we would imagine.

Transactional leaders can often get quick results, but often those are at the cost of relationships and in their wake they leave crushed spirits, hopes, and dreams.

Striving toward reaching your greatest potential is not for the faint-hearted. But if we make a start and keep a good tempo, inch by inch we will move toward reaching our greatest potential, and there is no telling what is in store for us along that journey! Becoming a transformational leader will quite possibly be the hardest thing you have ever done, but it might also be one of the most rewarding things you ever do.

TRAIN TO BE CLUTCH

- Write down 3-6 things you are willing to commit to doing today to close the gap between who you are and who you want to become. Make them specific. Put a time you will daily commit to each of them.
- Write out how you *feel* before you do your training. You may not *feel* great. But laugh and say, *"I choose to ignore my feelings and stick to my principles and commitments."*
- It should be hard. Strength is only built through resistance. Planes take off against the wind.

CHAPTER 16

OUR CERTAINTY > THEIR UNCERTAINTY

"I ASSUME YOU killed it, but how do you think you did?"

That text brought big tears to my eyes as I was overcome with emotion. It came from one of my mentors, Skip Grossman, after I had given the first keynote of my life at Pepperdine University.

Oftentimes people in leadership positions use their power and influence to really challenge those they lead. I'm not saying this is bad, but I think we have to be careful we aren't pushing people right into the fixed mindset and creating a need for them to *prove* themselves.

I think transformational leadership is about believing in people EVEN more than they believe in themselves. Our certainty MUST be greater than their uncertainty. They need to feel we believe in their ability to tackle the problem, overcome the obstacle, and defeat the odds.

The transformational leaders in my life have always believed in me even when I didn't believe in myself, AND even when my track record might have indicated good reason not to believe in me.

TRAIN TO BE CLUTCH

- Who believed in you when you didn't even fully believe in yourself?
- Who created a desire in you for you to prove yourself?
- Which type of leader do you want to be?

SOMETIMES THERE IS METHOD TO THE MADNESS

MY TEAM WAS in the middle of a two-game road trip on the west coast. We were driving in 3 minivans from Las Vegas to Utah when we pulled off the highway to refuel. I was following the van in front of me as we pulled into the gas station and there were 3 pumps in a row all open and waiting. Instead of stopping at the empty pump, the guy who coached our team was driving the lead van whipped around the corner, made us weave through a bunch of cars and pedestrians so that we could get to the single pump on the other side.

All the guys in the back of my van got angry and started hurling abuse at him for making such a ridiculous decision. They talked about the unusual placing of his head in relation to his backside and swore that they would have made a better decision.

I will admit, the decision he made puzzled me too, but I shrugged my shoulders and decided to see how this one played out. All the guys jumped out of the van and walked into the store while laughing together about how stupid and ridiculous the guy coaching was.

I jumped on Twitter while my van was refueling and once the tank was full I pulled around to the other side of the gas station to get out of the way. As the guys all piled in I smiled and waited for the right moment.

Out of love, and with a little smile, I told them to look to the right. As it turned out, the pumps he decided to drive past were pumps that only accepted membership cards.

After a moment of embarrassed silence, we all began laughing as the guys in the back removed their feet from their mouths!

The funny thing is that had he chosen those pumps, the guys in the back would have hurled the same abuse because he didn't realize that they were member-only pumps!

You see, I have learned over the years that those who lead, coach, and parent often make decisions that seem ridiculous to many people who aren't standing in their shoes. But oftentimes there is method to the madness.

I am not saying that in *every* situation we should sit back and watch how things play out, but I would strongly suggest giving people in leadership the benefit of the doubt as they make decisions. Sometimes there is method to the madness and it may take weeks to see how it plays out. But if we look at their decisions with the belief that they are incompetent and thoughtless, we will never learn from the situation.

I cannot tell you how many people serving as assistant coaches reach out to me complaining about how and why their boss makes decisions. I get it. Some of them sound ridiculous. Maybe you *would* do things differently. Maybe you *do* need to step up and say something. But do this before you draw conclusions.

Fill in the blank:
My boss is _____.

If what you wrote or thought is based on what that person has done and not on who he/she is, then chances are you are not in a good place to make a move.

Maybe you *would* do things differently. But 5 years down the road you might see that there was method to the madness all along.

Oftentimes, there is not a right or wrong way to do things. It's usually about what is most beneficial. All of us who are in positions of leadership have someone else who we report to, and often times we completely disagree with their decisions. However, one day you will be sitting in similar shoes, and even if you make decisions that are not the best, you will want those you lead to support your decision.

Remember, transformational leadership is about controlling what is under your control, and not wasting energy on things that aren't. You always have the option to quit, so either quit, or support those you are serving because they have a *very* tough job.

CHAPTER 18

CUE CARD

A GUY WHO coaches at the D-1 level contacted me one day because he was being pursued by a big name school to serve in their head coaching position.

I'll never forget something he said to me:

"I can't believe that out of the whole country they want me! I mean, I have one year of head coaching experience and our record last season was 14-18. I always thought that my progress in the coaching ranks was dependent on my wins and losses. But I have realized it's more about *my character.*"

That's it! Everyone needs to hear that!

CHARACTER > RESULTS

It's easy to have character when things are going how you want, but it is in the fire of trials where deep character is revealed & refined.

Without character, success or failure will eventually make you crumble.

"Anyways Jamie, they asked me about what I do that made such a big change in my life and coaching and I told them about you and our time together."

"What do you think had the greatest impact on you?" I asked.

"Definitely making reading a priority, even if it was only 20 minutes a day. I think another massive shift came from writing out a cue card."

I'll never forget sitting in his office midway through the season last year and seeing him flail his arms saying, "The girls are just *pouting* Jamie. *They're* just pouting." I wish I had video taped him that day, because in that very moment he was modeling the *EXACT* same behavior he was frustrated with them about!

Another guy he respected in coaching agreed with me and told him that his body language had really gone south. So my friend began writing out a cue card before he would go out to the floor.

On this card he wrote out what his most beneficial body language looked like regardless of what was happening in the game. He also wrote out phrases that he wanted to stick to that were growth oriented, NOT outcome oriented.

As his team made a run toward the end of the season, he told me that he would simply put his hands in his pocket, feel the edges of his index card, and it would kick his training into gear.

Every girl I have talked to on the team said that their run came as a result of the changes they could *feel* in him according to his verbal and non-verbal communication.

Is it really as simple as writing it down?

Yes, and no.

Writing it down is a start, but it needs to be something we are consciously practicing throughout the day.

Putting pen to paper is being proactive about doing things that are preparing us to respond and act in the most beneficial ways possible. It is priming our brains to act according to how our 'best self' would act.

Isn't that what we hope the people we lead are doing as we go through scouting reports? Isn't that what we hope our team is doing as we review the information for the presentation we are about to give?

If that's what we expect of those we lead, maybe we should model that ourselves.

So what goes on this cue card?

A number of things can be written and rehearsed, but here are some non-negotiables in our opinion.

YOUR PERSONAL MISSION-

Through all of his research, Daniel Pink says in his book *Drive,* that "the most deeply motivated people—not to mention the most productive and satisfied—hitch their desires to a cause larger than themselves." Remember, a mission is about who you are becoming; not what you want to achieve.

One of Joshua's is to become love so that everywhere he goes people will want what he has. Another personal mission of his is to be able to get diagnosed with terminal cancer and it not change a thing about how he lives. These help him regain perspective in trying times and help him remember to put first things first and trust Jesus.

BENEFICIAL BODY LANGUAGE-

Think about what will be the most useful posture, facial expression, and body language if and when adversity hits you and your group. Think

of the non-verbals from other people in leadership who you admire. Be careful not to equate *effective* with *most beneficial.* Yes staring one of your people down and injecting fear in their life may be effective, but is most likely not transformational.

CONSTRUCTIVE COMMUNICATION-
What key phrases will you use to guide your team in the midst of an unfavorable circumstance? Using questions, in our opinion, is most effective.

BENEFICIAL SELF-TALK-
What key words or phrases can you use to calm yourself down or build yourself up when things are not necessarily going as planned? What can help you keep things in perspective? It could be a quote, one word, a lyric, or even a prayer. Trying many different phrases throughout your day is a helpful way to find something meaningful to you.

WHAT'S YOUR NUMBER-
Thinking about the Warrior Dial, which will be explained in a later chapter, what is the number between 1-10 that you think reflects the emotional state in which you operate best?

Again, the cue card is not the magic dust that is going to radically transform you overnight. Like shooting free throws, it is a small piece that when practiced and utilized over and over consistently for a *significant* amount of time will bring massive changes in how you operate and who you become.

Remember, the main thing in coaching, leading, and parenting is not the outcome, but who we become in the process.

CHAPTER 19

GREATNESS IS FAR FROM SEXY

Greatness is far from sexy.
Mainly it is dirty work.
Sometimes it is the hardest work.
It's often boringly repetitive.
And it's always a huge responsibility.

Don't believe the hype.
Grab a broom and go to work.
Everyone thinks they want greatness,
Until they see what greatness requires.

"I've got a theory that if you give 100% all the time, somehow things will just work out in the end." –Larry Bird

TRAIN TO BE CLUTCH

- Would you be willing to never win if you were guaranteed to be transformational in every person's life you ever had the privilege of leading?
- Would you be willing to engage in 25 years of meaningful and intentional relationship even if a person never trusted Jesus with their life?

CHAPTER 20

JUST ENOUGH

HERE IS THE effect of a results-driven culture:

One of the guys I train called me one night a little frustrated and tired. He was in the middle of his preseason doing 3 practices per day with his team *and* staying on top of his reading, what went well journal, and visualization. He had honestly put in more work than anyone I've trained over a 3-month period. His perspective and mindset had grown considerably. But questions and doubts started to flood his mind.

"Jamie, I have a question that I feel weird asking you. We are doing 3 practices a day and I have been working harder than ever. In the first 2 practices I have left more on the field than I ever have before. I am pushing harder than I think is possible and I know I am growing. But, when we get to the night session I am struggling. It's a technical session and I haven't been executing very well because I am at the point of exhaustion by the end of the night."

"So what's your question?" I asked.

"Well, I'm wondering if I should do just enough in the first 2 sessions so that I can execute well in the technical session? I mean I am afraid that if I don't execute right now, then I won't play."

I took a deep breath, and asked "So are you asking if I think you should take some reps off so you make the starting 11? That's like me asking....do you think I should take steroids so I can get bigger faster?!"

As soon as he asked me the question I thought of a deep-seated belief that was sown in me when I was younger. A well-meaning man who coached me in youth soccer shared this advice when I was entering my freshman year of college:

"Jamie, make sure that during preseason you don't kill yourself in the running or the drills. You have to be able to play at nights if you want to make the starting 11."

Maybe that was one of the reasons why my focus for the first 15 years of my playing career was on doing just enough to beat other guys on my team and get a starting spot.

My focus was not on excelling, becoming the best I could be, and pushing others around me, because excelling required giving my very *very* best all of the time.

In fact, pursuing excellence could get in the way of me looking great at times, and it would require me to pursue failure while operating at the edges of my ability continually. Worst of all, it would require me to stop caring how I looked in everyone else's eyes.

If starting or performance is what is valued, pursuing excellence and daily growth is often pushed to the low end of the totem pole.

As I get to share my story with thousands of people across the country and hear the struggles they are having, I find it amazing that almost all of us are in a similar position.

We are afraid to stand out for the right reasons, and therefore we pursue fitting in for the wrong reasons.

We give lip service to giving 110% and leaving everything on the field, court, or track. In fact, that is what plenty of people in coaching *say* they are looking for, but what they ***really value*** are those who can produce results regardless of the process and effort. And for the record, **there is no such thing as 110% so stop saying it. It is confusing.**

So I said to my man Lucas, "Dude, if you grind the way you have, you are doing yourself and your team the greatest service. You are going to raise your level over the next few weeks to the point that you can last much longer than you ever have. People will either be inspired or sick of your effort. You will be like Rudy who got a bunch of heat from his buddy for standing out. But as he continued his pursuit to give everything on every rep, he raised the level of the guys around him. Moreover, he affected countless lives even though he only touched the field for a few seconds. Not to mention that character you are building will serve as a model for your family and those you engage with later on in life. The choice is yours though."

I'm not going to tell you what is right or wrong. But years from now, if you look your son or daughter in the face and tell them to give everything they have, you better have modeled it for them.

What does giving your very *very* best look like?

- Maybe it's sprinting *through* every line not *to* every line.
- Maybe it's instituting a policy of "You don't read. You don't play."
- Maybe it's starting to write the book you have always wanted to write.
- Maybe it's spending your weekend preparing for the meeting instead of chilling with your friends.

If you are currently leading in any capacity please pay close attention:

If results are valued, I can give you results.
You want grades? I can cheat or just memorize the information.
You want wins? You can beat me with a stick to run harder and faster.
You want sales? I'll be the pushiest or most cunning person on the floor.

These strategies can provide results in the short term, but at what cost?

In the book, *Drive*, Daniel Pink writes about some of the potential costs:

"Carrots and sticks can achieve precisely the opposite of their intended aims. Mechanisms designed to increase motivation can dampen it. Tactics aimed at boosting creativity can reduce it. Programs to promote good deeds can make them disappear. Meanwhile, instead of restraining negative behavior, rewards and punishments can often set it loose—and give rise to cheating, addiction, and dangerously myopic thinking.....tangible rewards tend to have a substantial negative effect on intrinsic motivation. When institutions focus on the short-term and opt for controlling people's behavior, they do considerable long-term damage."

If we are simply valuing the result, the grade, the sale, or the compliant behavior, we are equipping people with the mindset that they must be pushed, pulled, and prodded to do things that need to be done.

- We are conditioning people to operate out of fear, not love.
- We are telling them to value the results, rather than the process.
- We are telling them their worth comes from what they do.

Remember!!! True Mental Toughness is:

Having a great attitude
Giving your very *very* best

Treating people very very well
Being unconditionally grateful
Regardless of your circumstances.

I'm not saying that this is right or wrong, but I challenge you to ask yourself: ***What is most beneficial?***

"Talent is never enough. With few exceptions the best players are the hardest workers." -Magic Johnson

CHAPTER 21

WE REINFORCE WHAT WE VALUE

THE MAJORITY OF people who coach college golf have a very simple system for determining who plays in the lineup for each tournament. It is called qualifying.

They will play one or two qualifying rounds for a certain number of spots, and whoever shoots the best score travels to compete for their team. Sometimes the coaches leave one or two picks for themselves, but the rest of the spots come down to a result.

This is one of the main reasons we are advising the people who lead these teams to STOP the madness. How can you tell a kid that what you really value is true mental toughness and who you become as a result of golf, BUT then determine who gets to play completely based off of results?! It makes no sense, and the kids you lead KNOW exactly what you *truly* value.

You can treat people horribly, have awful body language, be grateful for nothing, and never give close to your best, BUT if you shoot one of the lowest numbers you are rewarded with representing your team.

We don't think you should scrap qualifying all together, but we think it should only be a small part of the equation, not the whole enchilada.

We think that there should be a clear understanding of character traits that are observed by the leadership and factor in heavily in the decision process. At the very least, these 4 should be heavily considered:

- Attitude
- Gratitude
- Effort
- How you treat others
- Self-Talk
- Body Language

Now for some of you, you might be saying, well I don't coach golf, so this doesn't apply to me, but what we have found is that almost all leaders have some system very similar to qualifying.

Take an honest assessment of your system and examine where and how you could be undermining all the process teaching you have been doing. Where and how do you reinforce that the results are what are truly valued in your organization?

If you want to become a transformational leader you must constantly be analyzing your system to make sure you are rewarding and valuing the process and who people become in the process.

CHAPTER 22

LET IT BURN

I WAS RECENTLY talking to a woman who coaches at the Division 1 level and she was telling me that one of her biggest issues is that she really does not trust that if she gives her team 10 minutes of autonomy in practice that they will use it well. She said that one of her biggest issues is looking at the girls and believing that they will be able to exercise self-control and get the most out of that time.

And so I said to her, "I want you to operate out of trust that the girls will use that time well, that they have the *ability* to exercise self-control, and trust that they <u>will fail</u> and <u>will abuse</u> it at some point. But I want you to continue to love them unconditionally."

One of the things we have to remember is that teams are going to get it wrong, people are going to overstep boundaries, and we need to let that happen because that's where a growth mindset is truly fostered.

John Kay shares this fantastic little story in his book *Obliquity*. The National Park Service is the governing body that looks after forest management here in the U.S. For a long time their policy was to extinguish all fires as quickly as possible. After some time in thought, they set a mandate in 1972 that they would only put out man-made fires, but allow natural fires to burn under scrupulous management.

Sixteen years later a huge forest fire swept through Yellowstone National Park and started to burn up huge masses of land. Now when the fire was done what they realized was that areas where these small

70

fires had been created in the past were the very areas where the large fire did not roll through. Why? **Because the small fires created a fire-break that kept the big fires from getting out of control.**

What can we learn from this?

Small mistakes and failures, individually or within the team, are actually healthy and good. I want my teams to regress in small, more manageable ways so they can learn, feel our trust and love in the tough times, and operate out of a growth mindset moving forward.

The more that we create small opportunities for autonomy where we can show our team that we trust them, the more they can begin to operate out of love in trying to grow into their greatest potential, rather than operating out of fear of making mistakes. They will learn to make better decisions when we are equipping them with the ability to make good decisions. Many of the people we work with feel like they don't have a choice.

If we foster this autonomy in our team what we start to develop are people who can exercise self-control and can self-regulate *because they want to, not because they have to.* In that environment people who coach and lead don't have to bitch, beg, prod or pull. All we have to do is model, guide, direct, and enforce healthy boundaries.

If you feel like you've been pushing, pulling, bitching, and begging what I would ask you to do is create a small piece of your practice, maybe something like 10 to 15 minutes very regularly in the middle of practice where you give the team *structured* autonomy. Tell the team that this is their time to get better at whatever they wish, and you trust that they will make good decisions and that you are there to help facilitate if they want help.

I know you might be thinking: "They're not going to use the time effectively or they're going work on things that are not most beneficial.

They need to work on some of their weaknesses, not what they *want* to work on!"

Please please please do not step in and try to change this! It is *their* time for autonomy. Let them work on what *they* want. If you try to direct their autonomy without being asked you are showing that you do not trust them and their ability to grow.

You need to sit back exuding and modeling the fact that you trust they will get something out of it because, after all, *they are building their own house.*

It's estimated that about half of *Google's* new offerings are created in these times of autonomy. They call them FedEx days where people are encouraged to work on whatever ideas they have even if they are not tech-related and deliver a finished product the next day. They are finding that when people feel they have control over their time, they make better decisions with their time.

This time is really about them putting tangible action on the belief that they are the people, flesh and blood, that have the most say about their life.

On a team of 30 people last year there was only one person who stuck to his 20 minutes of autonomy extra training throughout the season. When I came midway through the season to work with the team, who do you think was the one person that everybody had the most confidence in? It was that one guy who stuck to his process.

He was doing a drill for 20 minutes that was so fundamental that 5 year-olds do it. He was dribbling through 20 cones that were about 2 or 3 feet apart and then hitting the ball into a net 20 yards away. Was it completely functional for his position as a defender? No. But, the fact that he stuck with the process brought confidence to him, helping him believe he had the ability to control his body and the ball. What he told me was that his confidence in this area was actually trickling over to give him confidence in the rest of his game.

You've got to remember autonomy is not just about the skill, it's about developing the belief in those you lead that you trust them and that they can trust their training.

And what you can start to do is step back, direct, and mentor.

Small fires will arise. Let them burn.

TRAIN TO BE CLUTCH

- Reflect on the last season, month, quarter or even week. What small fires could you have let burn? How could letting them fail have actually been a good thing?
- Try giving your team 10-15 minutes regularly to work on things they choose to work on at practice or in the office.
- If you work from home or parent, plan the same amount of time to work on something that excites you.

CHAPTER 23

BE HERE NOW

I WAS DIAGNOSED "ADHD" when I was in high school and one of my biggest challenges in life has always been keeping my feet and my mind in the same building.

One of the most powerful things a person in leadership can do is be present. I mean TRULY present, not present in body, but absent in mind, spirit, and heart.

When we are fully present and fully engaged we multiply our skill, impact, and our time and effort.

So often we lose time because we aren't present and therefore our work suffers, requiring more time.

Or,

We aren't present at home or with our kids, and then that ends up creating more challenges for us down the road.

Transformational leadership is making a commitment to becoming more present and fully engaged in everything we do.

As you start to develop this skill you will notice yourself acquiring more of your most precious resource, time, every day.

"I often reminded the players to focus on the journey rather than the endgame, because if you give the future all your attention, the present will pass you by." — Phil Jackson, *Eleven Rings: The Soul of Success*

TRAIN TO BE CLUTCH

- What is the device that keeps you from being present?
- How can you create pockets of time with it off or completely silent so you can get better at being present where your feet are?
- What are you willing to commit to doing to develop this skill?
- What are you willing to sacrifice to be more present in all the places that matter most?
- I always have my phone on 100% silent, not even vibrate, so that I won't be interrupted by it when I am with a person.

CHAPTER 24

MY ISSUE WITH KNOWING YOUR *WHY*

MANY PEOPLE WHO write books and give lectures on tapping into your greatest potential tell you that you must start with "Why". They say you must know your "why." And that if you have a big enough "why" you can conquer any "*how.*"

I will give you 2 quick arguments from a scientific perspective and then from a Biblical perspective on my problems with this advice.

First scientifically. If neuroscientists agree that your conscious brain is unaware of over 99.99% of what your brain is processing on a second-by-second basis, then how can we ever know "why" we do what we do?[5] We can make educated guesses, or we can hope we do something for some noble purpose, but I don't think we can ever truly know why.

I had the privilege to study under David Rubin at Duke, who is arguably the second foremost expert in the world on autobiographical memory. What the top experts in this field have shown is that our memories are not actually shaped by what happened. Our memories are actually shaped by the stories we tell about what happened, and every time we access and retell the memory it gets re-written again.

---

5 Brain Works, The mind-bending science of how you see, what you think, and who you are. Michael S. Sweeney. National Geographic

Moreover, in 2000, NYU researchers Joseph LeDoux and Karim Nader discovered that they could erase memories by tinkering with retrieval and storage. It seems clear that our memories are in fact *our* memories, not necessarily what actually happened.

So, if our memories are *actually* formed through the *retelling* of events, and if we are only consciously aware of a minuscule amount of what our brain is processing, then how can we ever truly know why we do what we do? My argument is that we cannot.

Secondly, the Scriptures say, "The heart is deceitful above all things, and desperately sick; who can understand it?" (*NIV* Jeremiah 17:9) Furthermore, it adds, "All the ways of a man are pure in his own eyes, but the Lord weighs the spirit." (*ESV* Proverbs 16:2)

"Knowing your why" might make you sleep better at night, but I think it can also lead to questionable behaviors on the journey. If you have a big enough why, you can justify almost any questionable behavior. If you have a big enough why, you can rationalize any means to your end.

"There seems to be a sense in which people in leadership can always justify their plans and goals as good and right....Thus equipped we are capable of transforming even the most selfish motivated action into an act of sacrificial altruism in our own minds." - Gary L. McIntosh & Samuel D. Rima Sr. "Overcoming the Dark Side of Leadership"

Here is something better than a *why*. I believe you should create a mission that is bigger than yourself, that is controllable, that you can start today and don't need permission for. But you don't need a "why."

MOVE FROM GENERAL TO SPECIFIC

ONE OF MY favorite actors growing up was Jim Carrey. A scene that still makes me laugh comes from *Liar, Liar* when he is in the bathroom trying to figure out how he can convince the judge to give him a continuance so as to buy some time in his trial. He has a problem however, he cannot lie because of a wish his son made.

By hitting his head on the wall he comes up with the brilliant plan of beating himself up and making it seem as though he was mugged. And so ensues a minute of him beating the crap out of himself!

When another person walks into the bathroom and asks what he is doing, he says, "I'm kicking my ass, do you mind!!!!"

If we are honest, I think a lot of us do some inadvertent ass-kicking to ourselves. I know I did, and I have to be aware and intentional not to do it anymore!

I was talking with a young woman the other day and she had just returned from a retreat with a large group. I asked her one of my favorite questions, "What did you learn from that trip?" (You'd be amazed at how many people have trouble or cannot answer that question!)

She took a long pause and said, "I realized I am not spending enough time with God." Probably because of the influence from Joshua, in my mind I said, "I'm going to stop you there because I have something more important to tell you."

I interjected, "Tell me what is *enough* time with God?" She paused and smiled knowing that there is no time allotment that will satisfy or make Him love us more. That's the whole thing about His extravagant love and grace!

But I was really trying to touch on this idea of *doing enough* in all aspects of life.

When I was growing up I had huge dreams that I wanted to live out in soccer. I spent thousands of hours practicing and watching the game. I missed out on many extracurricular experiences because of my commitment to growing. But even with all that training, I always had this thought in my mind that I was not doing enough.

At times, the feeling and belief that I was not living up to some ridiculous standard was eating me alive inside. I felt like Jim Carey stepping on my own toes, punching myself in the face, putting soap in my eyes, and slamming my head between the toilet bowl and seat:

- *"Jamie your first touch sucks."*
- *"Jamie you need to put in more hours."*
- *"Zach is doing more sit-ups than you right now."*
- *"Your time isn't good enough on your 3 mile run."*
- *"Jamie you're not good enough."*

Sound familiar?

Because I was so general, my training was not as effective as it could have been. Moreover, I beat myself into feeling like a worthless person.

One of my greatest passions is to help people move from general to specific. It's one thing to say you want to spend *more* time with God, but what is an amount of time you can commit to reading, writing, or prayer? That's specific.

Instead of saying I want to become an excellent soccer player, I would encourage my younger self to write out 4 keys components of my game I was going to work on for a particular amount of time that week.

Instead of saying you want to read more books, how many pages can you commit to reading every day?

Instead of saying you need to spend more time researching the company, how many hours can you commit to that research this week?

Instead of saying you need to be better at public speaking, how many hours will you commit this month to watching great speakers and practicing at home?

What is really cool to watch and experience is the empowerment one feels when they write out exactly what they are going to commit to.

It's not rocket science.
It's not impossible.
It's really simple.
But we have to exercise self-control.

Moving from general to specific not only narrows our focus on how we are going to improve or execute, but it helps us jump out of the self-laid trap of not doing enough.

TRAIN TO BE CLUTCH

- What are your *enoughs* right now? List them out. Choose 2-4 of them and make a commitment list for each one.
- In what areas do you find yourself telling those you lead that they aren't good enough? Instead, tell them how you can see them operating in that context if they focus on commitments.

CHAPTER 26

NEW NORMAL

"HAVE YOU ALWAYS been so calm and reserved?" I asked knowing that I had to choose my words wisely! He served as a Navy SEAL for crying out loud!!!

He told me that he has always been kind of quiet in conversations, but "overall, I have a new normal."

This guy had been through 2.5 years of some of the most intense training on the planet. During Hell Week he ran over 100 miles, did more than 20 hours of exercises a day, and only slept for 4 hours within a 5 day period! And who knows what he went through while fighting Al Qaeda!

By the way, thank you to everyone who has served, is serving, or is family to those who serve in the military. Sincerely, thank you!

He continued, "There could be a bomb dropped on the building next to us and you and Cam would run and hide. I probably wouldn't move, then after a few seconds I would become energized and do something. That is my normal now."

I'd like to believe all of my own mental training would prove him otherwise, but if I'm honest, he's probably right.

I loved that phrase: *new normal.*

As I reflect back on my life I have realized that the toughest challenges helped me create new normals. Before college, my lifting workouts were pretty static but hard. Then I embraced coach Davis' circuit lifting and the new normal was to puke, or at least come close, during weights.

I remember I had a whole semester to read a novel in one of my undergrad history classes and I felt like I didn't have enough time to read it all. Now, married, a dad, working, and training I finish books almost every week, and have even completed multiple books in one day multiple times.

Most of us fail to reach a new normal because we do not consistently operate on the edges of our ability. Within a 2-hour practice we go hard most reps, but we don't go as hard as we can until the last few minutes.

Most of us produce ridiculous amounts of content right before the deadline, and very little in the weeks or days proceeding.

When it comes down to it, many of us practice conservation.

This marked my training in soccer most of my life. I would conserve energy throughout practice so that I could last the whole session. But because I focused on managing my fitness, I never really expanded my fitness as far as it could go.

One person who blows my mind is JJ Watt. He has to be taken out sometimes during a defensive set because he is so out of breath from the previous 6 plays. I consistently see him on the sidelines, on one knee, and breathing like he just finished a marathon. But then he stands up and gets back at it. *He wasn't born the way he is now.*

This man who served as a Navy SEAL was not born with the ability to sit through a bombing raid. I was not reading books weekly, or even at all, during my high school education.

In each of these cases, and many others, we find people who sought out tough challenges again and again so that they could thrive in most situations.

"My training," he confided, "was so hard that live battle felt like a training mission."

What's your normal right now?

In what ways can you start to operate on the edges of your ability?

Every day we are presented with countless opportunities to create new normals in our life. We asked one of our clients to write an article every single day, and out of that he created new normal for himself.

We don't need any fancy training program to do it. We can focus on creating new normals in how we treat people when we are tired, choosing unconditional gratitude when our circumstances suck, opting for a growth mindset in the face of challenges and failures, or just consistently giving our very best instead of doing just enough.

I don't want normal in my life. *Normal looks like it sucks, so I am going to keep pushing the edges of my ability to create 'new normals' in the areas of how I treat people, the effort I give, my mindset, my finances, my relationships, and my work.*

TRAIN TO BE CLUTCH

- What is your current normal in the following categories:
  - How I treat others when I'm tired
  - How much I rest
  - How often I ask questions

- How much I give
- My dominant mindset
- Time toward my significant relationships
- Healthy living
- Reading
- What would you like your new normal to be for each of these?
- Which 2 categories can you make a priority this month?

CHAPTER 27

OPERATING OUT OF FEAR OR LOVE?

Someone asked me why I stopped playing soccer recently.
Did I have a great time? Absolutely.
Was it difficult? You bet.
But I knew what was most beneficial.

I MUST HAVE been the only person in the casino holding a Bible and a journal that day. Or maybe any day! I was walking back up to my room when one of the guys who coaches our team saw me and asked what I was doing. I told him "I read, pray, and write most mornings. It's usually when I make most of my big decisions."

"Did you make any decisions today?" he asked.

"Yeah, we need to talk," I responded.

I had decided that morning that I was going to step away from playing soccer. It wasn't a split decision and it certainly wasn't easy.

I never thought that day would come, but there it was. I told him that I was not giving my best to my family, I wasn't giving my best to those I train, and I was not giving my best to excelling in soccer. Something had to give, and I knew it was soccer.

He heard what I was saying, but wasn't thrilled about it. We had just finished a road trip and had home games two days later. With a few guys injured and the team feeling a little discouraged from past results, my absence would most likely be felt.

As I said, he respected my decision, but he asked me to play in the next 2 games. I thought and prayed about it for a while. I was just about to text him when a great question came to mind: *Am I operating out of fear or love?*

You see, I was about to text and say that I was going to play. I know it sounds like the noble or *right* thing to do, but it was clear that I would be operating out of fear if I played. I wasn't going to play because I wanted to fight alongside my teammates or honor my commitment. I was going to do it so that he and everyone else would think well of me. I was fearful about what he would say to others about my character. *And it was at that moment I realized I had been operating out of fear most of my life.*

I explained my decision to him and said I was going to step away. As hard as that was, I decided to live by my principles instead of my feelings. I operated out of love, not fear. I chose to spend time with my family because I wanted to, and because it is one of my highest priorities, not because I was fearful of what my wife Amy would think.

As I said, I noticed that I had been operating out of fear most of my life. I had been living in direct opposition to the biblical truth that **"God has not given us a spirit of fear, but one of power, *love*, and self-control." (*ESV* 2 Tim 1:7)**

I realized that much of what I did in life was dominated by fear.

Sometimes I would only wash my hands out of fear that someone might hear that the water in the sink was not running. That's ridiculous! I should be washing my hands because I want to and I know its healthy for me and my family.

Sometimes I would only go out and practice on my own because I was fearful that if I didn't then another kid out there would have the upper hand on me.

I was doing homework because I was fearful of not getting into the college that I wanted, rather than seeking wisdom and using my circumstances to help me excel in life.

I was picking out the clothes I would wear to school based off of my fear of not fitting in.

I was doing just enough in practice so as not to stand out for making mistakes or trying extremely hard, rather than running my butt off to make myself and the team better.

I am not saying that we only do things that we *feel* like doing. No, I want you to operate according to principles not feelings. But *doing things out of a heart of fear and compulsion is not nearly as effective as doing things out of love.*

I do the dishes quite often in my house. I don't ever *feel* like doing them. It is not easy, and quite frankly I hate it. But as often as I can, I do the dishes during the day so that Amy doesn't have to do them. If the kitchen is clean, then she has an extra 20 minutes to sleep, read, or whatever while our son naps. I do it because I love Amy and I want to bless her. I also do it knowing that completing the dishwashing process gives me energy to create new content. I know it's weird, but that's what happens.

As we begin to switch from operating out of fear and move toward operating out of love, we begin to change our *have to's to get to's*. We move from relying on extrinsic motivation to operating from intrinsic

motivation. We begin to work with energy, passion, and commitment, not because anyone told us we had to, but because we can.

Please, play your sport because you want to play, not because you want your parents or anyone else to think well of you.

Dress the way you want to dress, not according to what *you* think others will think of you.

If you feel that your company's strategies are unethical or misguided, don't just stay for the money and benefits.

Operate out of love and enjoy the freedom.

Love attracts energy.
Fear consumes it.

CHAPTER 28

SOMEBODY IS ALWAYS WATCHING

I HAD ONE of the fiercest internal struggles of my life recently. My 21-month-old son and I were out at the driving range hitting our wedges and were working through a large bucket of balls. Now out of the 30 balls he hit, he probably hit 28 about 15 yards ahead.

I had hit all of my balls and JJ only had about 10 left. The first one he duffed and it just barely trickled across the rope. He started moving toward it to pick it up, and I said, "JJ let's leave it there bud. We don't cross the rope or else we could get hit." So he walked back, addressed another ball and stroked it.

I had a problem though: I couldn't stop looking at that ball by the rope. It was like watching someone eat an ice cream on a smoking hot day knowing you can't have one. All I wanted was to take that beautiful Titleist and put it 75 yards out onto the green with a 56-degree wedge!

I knew I could pull a fast one and tell JJ to look at the birdies in the sky and take it while he wasn't looking. Or I could just tell him that there are exceptions to be made. But I knew in my heart that he was soaking in *everything* I did more than everything I said.

I have the pleasure of training a woman who is one of the best in the world at her sport. Recently she has been on the bench due to a fierce battle for her position. Even before our time together she had an amazing heart and drive to excel. She has been working extremely hard on having a great attitude, giving her very best, treating people really well, and being unconditionally grateful regardless of her circumstances. But she still hasn't touched the field.

After a game the other day one of her teammates asked her how she does it.

"How do I do what?" she asked.

"How do you remain focused, ready, and have such a great attitude? You influence everyone of our games and *you aren't even on the field!*"

I've learned this: there is always someone watching. There is always someone who is taking their cues about life from the way we treat people and what we do.

- Maybe there's a chance that your supporting staff might read more if they saw you create margins in your day to read.
- Maybe your company's default language would change if you started focusing on engaging power questions and operating with linguistic intentionality.
- Maybe your team will increase their work ethic as they see you give your very very best daily in the office.

Someone is always watching.
Model the change you want to see.

CHAPTER 29

START EQUIPPING. STOP ENABLING.

HAVE YOU EVER used the phrases, "That's not good enough," "It's got to be better," or "Come on you're not getting it"?

When we hear these phrases it usually does cause us to try harder. But, in most sports, and a lot of areas of life, trying *harder* is not necessarily the best thing for us.

For instance, if you're working on improving your golf swing, trying harder usually results in poorer shots.

In track and field, people run faster when they run at 80-90%, then when they are trying to run 100%.

In soccer, if you're really struggling to hit the ball on target, usually the last thing you want to do is try to hit the ball harder.

What seems apparent is that just *trying harder* does not guarantee better results. In leadership it is very frustrating to say the same things over and over and over. I consistently hear people in coaching say that if they didn't have to coach effort, their job would be a lot easier.

So what's our default reaction in leadership? Punishment.

I was at a practice the other day and the guy who was coaching was really frustrated that the effort, focus, and end product were not reaching the desired standard. So he stopped practice and said "everybody get down and give me 20 push-ups!"

They started doing the drill again and it still wasn't up to the standard that he wanted. So he said "everybody on the line. If you don't want to put in the effort playing, we'll get the work in doing sprints."

Now, I know from years of experience in sports that when someone who is coaching stops practice and forces us to run because of a lack of effort or focus, we usually come back with much more energy and focus because we don't want to run again. It usually creates an immediate result. No doubt about it.

But here's the real question: does that translate into games?

When your team has really low energy in a game, we can't just stop play and say, "everybody give me push-ups" or "everybody get on the line and run." We're in the middle of a game! And because we have not *equipped* our teams to self-regulate, they turn to punishing each other in ways that sound similar to how they have been yelled at during practice. I know from experience that this can cause a team to implode.

Simply put: physical punishment does not equip.

What we need to do is equip people to regulate and train them to be able to adjust on-the-fly and create solutions in the run of play.

So how do we equip them?

I was training one of my guys in soccer this summer and we were doing a passing drill that was very simple and very fundamental. While he was doing the drill the energy level was not very high, it was very lethargic, and the end product was not very good.

So I asked him to stop and I calmly said, "On a scale of 1 to 10 I want you to rate your energy level in that last drill. 1 being very very very slow and 10 being extremely high strung and fast as possible."

"I think I was at about a 3 or 4," he said.

I said, "Yea that sounds about right. So here's what we will do. Let's do it again for 30 more seconds and this time I want you to operate at like a 10. Go as fast and as hard as you can."

So he began to do the drill going as fast as he could. Once he finished I said, "Now I want you to operate at a 7 or 8."

When he finished we came back together. I smiled and asked him when he thought he played his best. He admitted it was when he tried to reach a 7 or 8. And I agreed:

"The first time we did it we were operating at 4 and there wasn't a lot of energy, you were not being athletic, and the ball was going everywhere.

When you operated at a 10 you were off-balance, struggling to breathe, and the ball wasn't hitting the target.

But, when you operated at a 7 or an 8 everything changed. You dropped into an athletic position, you made your face with your eyes wide, you were breathing strong and controlled, and you were knocking the ball right back to my feet every single time. *That's your sweet spot.*"

3 minutes and he had a tool for life. Now when he and I get together and we do drills I don't have to say, "The effort isn't good enough," or "Hey it's gotta be better." I'm not giving him vague terms and I certainly don't want him to just try harder.

What I've done is I've equipped him with a number that is associated with a certain level of effort that feels a certain way. Now all I have to do when I go out to train him is say, "Hey what's your number?" And if he's doing the drill and he's not at that number all I need to do is ask the question "How would you rate yourself out of 1-10 in terms of energy in that last drill?" If he says, "Oh I was at a 4." All I have to ask is "Where do you need to be? Let's do it again." It's fascinating to watch.

Oh, and by the way, he's 9 years old!

By taking 3 minutes of our time I was able to settle down and equip him with a tool that allows him to self-regulate. He doesn't have to have someone who's pushing and pulling him or bitching and begging. All he has to do is ask himself, "What's my number? Where am I?"

Back to the guy who was coaching his team. Once I equipped him with this tool and he chose to employ it, he started to see an impact in a few of his guys. He didn't have to waste his breath and get angry and yell and try to motivate them. He asked a simple question. And what he is now doing is equipping his team to be able to self-regulate, exercise self-control, and create solutions on the field.

The cool thing is that this scale isn't just for energy. We can use it for

- Attitude
- Commitment
- Focus
- Effort

If we choose to use it, all we have to do intermittently throughout training and throughout games is say to them "What's your number in terms of focus? What's your number in terms of energy?"

If we really want to create a culture where people do things because they want to, where people really scratch and claw to operate on the edges of their ability, and if we are trying to create a culture where we don't have to coach effort, we need to start _equipping_ people to be able to self-regulate.

It may not happen as quickly as we would like, but at least this way we are equipping rather than begging or worse.

CHAPTER 30

STATE-BASED LEARNING

I HEAR IT from people who play high level sports all the time, **"I KNOW I can hit that shot! I do it all the time in training."**

I always ask them the same question, "Are you sure you have hit that shot in training?"

They usually say, "YES! Thousands of times!"

I then tell them about a bunch of drunken rats.

You see, a group of researchers got a group of lab rats drunk one day and then taught them how to navigate a maze. When the rats sobered up, they forgot how to run the maze. When the researchers got them drunk again they remembered how to navigate the maze, WITHOUT being re-taught.

This phenomenon is called "State-Based Learning."

Most of us are training in very different emotional, psychological, and physiological states than we operate in during competition.

We tell people who coach sports that are fast moving, reactionary sports such as basketball, soccer, and football, **your training should be so fast and hard that games actually slow down for your team.**

For deliberate, non-reactionary sports like golf, diving, and much of track & field, it is of great importance that we track and simulate similar heart rates to the rates we will experience at the highest levels of competition.

You might be able to easily hit hundreds of full 7 irons to inside 12 feet during practice, but if you are training with your heart rate at 100 beats per minute, and your heart rate gets up to 140-160 beats per minute in competition, then you actually haven't trained to execute that shot in competition.

Truthfully, you shouldn't even get upset when you don't hit it well, because your body is operating in a very foreign context.

It's like the difference between driving your vehicle around a *NASCAR* track with no one else out there and driving around the track with professionals who drive in *NASCAR* racing with you. The two are very similar, and at the same time, worlds apart.

There are simple things you can do to simulate a similar heart rate. Do some jumping jacks, a sprint, wall sits, or a few push-ups, before hitting your shots in training, and wear a heart rate monitor during training to know exactly where you are.

For those of us in leadership, we need to be thinking about how to make periods of training more difficult than what our teams will face in competition or in business dealings. I know we have already mentioned the replicating competition-level heart rates, but here are a few other ideas:

- Blare loud static on the speakers instead of the team's favorite playlist.
- Allow other people you lead to disrupt the person shooting the free throw.

- Don't allow the team to communicate verbally.
- Reduce the amount of time allowed to complete the presentation.
- Spray water on the person ready to putt.
- Create constraints in which they have to operate.

As we do this consistently we will begin to approach competition knowing that we are equipped to handle anything that is thrown at us.

CHAPTER 31

HOW GOOD IS GOOD ENOUGH?

"I hit my number.
I always thought when I hit my number I would be fulfilled.
I always thought that I would finally feel complete, satisfied, and secure in myself.....

BUT I FEEL just the same."

His number was $50 million.

Do you think more money will satisfy you?
Do you think more championships will satisfy you?
Do you think a bigger house, or nicer car will ever satisfy you?
Do you think that raise and new position will quiet that voice inside you saying you will never be good enough?
Do you think that next level of achievement will permanently quench that voice inside you telling you that you are a fraud and eventually everyone will find out?

When I say *satisfy*, I don't mean the temporary high you get from those things, I'm talking about a permanent, long-lasting, deep satisfaction. Do you think they will ever satisfy you?

"I have often said that I wish people could realize all their dreams, wealth, and fame so that they can see that it is not where you are going to find your sense of completion." -Jim Carrey

How good is good enough?

Do you think Geno Auriemma was ever satisfied at any point when his team at UCONN was 47-0?

Did he think the effort was ever good enough, the amount of sacrifice was ever good enough?

It's extremely rare to find people in leadership who are content.

What are we compensating for with our endless pursuit of the illusion of perfection?

What is suffering because of it?

It might be worth asking yourself, *"What is the current condition of my most important relationships?"*

Are you content with the people you get to lead? Or is there always more that is required of them?

Timothy Gallwey makes a great observation:

"When we plant a rose seed in the earth, we notice that it is small, but we do not criticize it as "rootless and stemless." We treat it as a seed, giving it the water and nourishment required of a seed. When it first shoots up out of the earth, we don't condemn it as immature and underdeveloped; nor do we criticize the buds for not being open when they appear. We stand in wonder at the process taking place and give the plant the care it needs at each stage of its development. The rose is a rose from the time it is a seed to the time it dies. Within it, at all times, it contains its whole potential. It seems to be constantly in the process of change; yet at each state, at each moment, it is perfectly all right as it is." —Timothy Gallwey, From the Inner Game of Tennis.

We love James Clear's reflection on this matter:

"Ambition and contentment are not opposites, but we often make the mistake of thinking that they are incompatible. On the one hand, experts tell us that we should be mindful, focused on the present, and content with our lives regardless of the results. On the other hand, coaches and champions tell us that successful people out-work everyone else, that we must never be satisfied, and that complacency is undesirable. The rose seed, however, is both content and ambitious. As Gallwey says, at no point are we dissatisfied with the current state of the rose seed. It is perfectly all right at each moment. Yet, it is also incredibly ambitious. The rose seed never stops growing. It is constantly seeking to get to the next level. Every day it is moving forward, and yet, every day it is just as it should be."[6] -James Clear

I ask again, ***how good is good enough?***

There is always room to grow, but do those you lead feel like nothing they do is ever good enough? Do they feel like they can never satisfy you? Do they feel like a weed among the roses?

Being content does not mean that you settle. You can be content and still be focused on learning and growing. But if we are not careful, we will crush or neglect the people we get to lead now, with one eye on those we want to lead in the future.

I want to inspire people to be the best they can be, but simultaneously make them feel loved and valued for who they are, right where they are.

I think we need to fight for contentment. We know we can do more, become more, and achieve more; that is a given. Everything is always

---

6 http://jamesclear.com/self-judgment

growing in one direction or the other. Comfortable should not be our aim, but contentment should be. Contentment is a deep peace in knowing we are actually where we are supposed to be at that exact moment. When we are there, we can do our best and rest well knowing our best *is* good enough.

TRAIN TO BE CLUTCH

- Write out the 5 people you interact most with in your team or organization. Next to their name, write out ways in which you are grateful for their presence.
- Write out your roster and do the same exercise. Choose a few people to give a specific and sincere compliment to.

WHAT WILL YOU *ACTUALLY* REMEMBER?

I WAS SITTING in the office with three ladies who currently coach at the Division 1 level when I asked a simple question:

"What are your most treasured memories from your time playing college ball?"

Silence. Eyebrows rising. (I'm training the ability to sit in silence and wait people out!)

Finally the silence ended as one lady said, "I don't know if this is good or not, but it was the trips with the team. Flights, hotels, and bus rides with the other girls."

AND she had won a BIG 10 championship.

The other two ladies nodded along sharing the exact same kind of moments. They all sort of chuckled, and then they realized, it's probably going to be the same for their girls.

It's not the top of the line training equipment we try to get, it's not the ridiculous tiger-head tunnel we spend thousands of dollars on for them to run out of, and it's not the championships they win or don't

win. *It's the relationships they develop and the memorable moments that will be treasured.*

Here's a guy who coaches and gets it. One of the people who had played for him told me about their run in the national tournament. It was being hosted at Disney World and the teams involved had a good portion of the park sectioned off just for their enjoyment. The day before the big game their coach didn't call a practice. He said, "Have fun!"

My friend who played on the team couldn't quite understand what he was up to. He told her it was simple. Years later he knew that the girls wouldn't remember what they did with their winners medals if they won, and they probably wouldn't be up at night thinking about what could have been if they lost. Some of those girls may never have had the chance to return to Disney, and none of them have had the chance to connect with each other in such a fun way.

As bad as we want to believe that holding the trophy, getting the bonus, or landing the dream client will be the most fulfilling thing in ours and others' lives, it most likely won't be.

On our deathbeds we will not wish we earned more money or won more games. We will wish that we loved and inspired more people.

As you move forward in becoming a transformational leader, focus on creating an environment that fosters and cultivates people and relationships.

CHAPTER 33

WORK SMARTER NOT JUST HARDER

SOME PEOPLE GET high off of grinding. They want to be the first in and the last out. They seemingly take pride in sleeping at the office and sacrificing temporal pleasures like time with family for the truly important things like making more money and winning more trophies (*Sarcasm emphasized*).

We believe in sacrifice, and hustle. We have written and spoken extensively on it, but **not all hard work is created equal.**

Take sports for example. Most people who coach use "block" practice as their main method of training. Block practice is doing a repetitive technique over and over again.

For example:

In basketball, catching and shooting from the same spot for 10 reps at a time.

In golf, hitting 25 seven iron shots in a row, or 25 three footers in a row.

In business one example was a guy who focused on creating more and more content every day instead of focusing on distributing the content to more and more people.

Basically what it comes down to is that we often are doing things that make us "feel" better instead of doing the hard work that makes us "get" better.

For many people who coach "block" practice is what they are comfortable doing, and they enjoy seeing people get better in the moment. "Random" practice, which is never doing the same reps over again, is very scary to them and it feels more unorganized and out of control. But studies have shown retention is sometimes double for groups using "random" practice than that of groups using "block" practice.

Ultimately we have to ask the tough question, **"Is this maximizing my growth or does it just make me feel better?"**

Getting in the gym might make you feel better, but you might be able to get more out of 25 minutes of deliberate random practice than 2 hours of going through the motions with block practice. You might be able to get more out of dividing that 2 hours up for sleep, what went well journals, visualization, highlight film study, and reading as well.

Staying late at the office and skipping out on paid vacations might make you feel better, but studies have shown those who rest and take their vacation actually perform better, get promoted more often, do better work, and are better compensated.

Don't just work harder, work smarter.

TRAIN TO BE CLUTCH

- Watch "Block v Random Practice: Optimizing Practice with Motor Learning" on YouTube

CHAPTER 34

TRUST YOUR GUT

IF YOU EVER sit down with your kid to play a video game you usually lose because they know the game. They have advanced knowledge of that guy that jumps out around the corner, and where all the shortcuts are.

It's wise to learn from people who know the road ahead, because history repeats itself in the markets, in civilization, and even in fashion.

We wrote a chapter in *Burn Your Goals* about the utmost importance of your inner circle. We talk about the importance of surrounding yourself with people who are wiser than you, and who have become who you want to become.

We also have written and spoken extensively about the importance of fueling your heart daily with wisdom from what you read, watch, and listen to.

However, after I seek out wise counsel, I always know to trust my gut.

Our brain is processing so much information per second that we are unaware of over 99.99% of it. Our subconscious often has access to information our conscious brain doesn't have, and our subconscious is always giving us a gut feeling about things.

If you have trusted your life to Jesus we believe you have the Holy Spirit inside of you that acts as your gut as well.

Rarely does my gut tell me to do the comfortable thing. Usually it tells me to do the really hard, often uncomfortable thing.

BUT KNOW THIS: My gut never is telling me to violate my principles, and usually it is telling me to live by my principles no matter the temporary cost.

Sometimes that is to give away a lot of money to a cause I believe in.

Sometimes that is to not fight the person who just sucker-punched me in the ear.

Sometimes that is to simply say I'm sorry.

One time that was to pass on scholarships to law school and move across the country into a homeless shelter to serve.

One time that was to not write my masters thesis and drop out of one of the most prestigious schools in the world.

Sometimes that is to tell a person in leadership, who has just brought me out to work with their program and who is in the hall of fame, some piece of hard truth that is going to sting.

Sometimes that is moving to a foreign country where you know no one because you felt God stirring your heart.

Sometimes it is speaking hard truth into darkness.

Sometimes that is stepping down from a prestigious position to chase a dream or calling that makes little to no sense in your mind.

Sometimes it is standing my ground to defend someone when I know it could cost me a job.

Sometimes it is resigning from a highly reputable position when I realize I would have to violate my principles to stay on.

The greater your leadership role the bigger the crowd, and consequentially the greater the temptation to follow or listen to the crowd.

When Lebron James moved to Miami to play for the Heat "the crowd" (media, fans, bloggers) all had an opinion on how he should and shouldn't lead. For a while it was obvious that he was losing sleep while reading about what the crowd thought he should be doing. He even took on the role of "the villain" for a little while, until he eventually realized he wasn't being his authentic self and trusting his gut.

Greatness takes time.
Greatness takes patience.

Nothing great was built fast enough for today's instant gratification society.

The crowd is always going to have an opinion, but I've found my best bet is to trust my gut. Not my feelings, not what I necessarily want to do, but my core conviction about which way I think I should go and what I should do. I've found it has never let me down, and when I haven gone against it is when I seem to get myself into the most trouble.

TRAIN TO BE CLUTCH

- When was a time when you went against your gut and it was a costly mistake?
- When was a time when you trusted your gut, even when it was unfashionable? Did you end up regretting it, or did your gut prove to be right in the long run?
- Remember that an opportunity is NOT an opportunity if it requires you to compromise your principles and integrity.

CHAPTER 35

YOU'VE LOST YOUR PRIVILEGE. SEE YOU TOMORROW.

I COULDN'T BELIEVE it. Everyone wanted to talk about the same challenge. It was the one person on the team who they could not encourage to put in great work.

Those coaching the team told me, "We don't know what to do. We try to encourage him, but when he doesn't put the work in the whole team has to run. Then they all get frustrated with him and he doesn't even try during *that* running." The guy serving as the lifting coach said the same thing. "How do we motivate him?

First of all, any person in a leadership role needs to read Daniel Pink's *Drive*. It is THE MUST read on motivation, and certain strategies you might be using could actually be squashing the intrinsic motivation of the people you lead.

My response was simple. "What does he love more than anything?"

"He loves to play ball," they all agreed.

"Awesome. Basketball is a privilege, not a right. Take away the opportunity for him to play."

Blank faces...

Here's the thing, what we know is that shouting is not working. Physical punishment is not bringing about any change other than creating an aversion to the very activity that will help any person grow in their sport. Something has to change.

So here is what we suggest. **Create, communicate, and ENFORCE healthy boundaries.** Set ridiculously high standards for things under one's control. When those boundaries are crossed and the standards are not met, it's simple: "You've lost your opportunity to get better with the team today. Go home. We'll see you tomorrow."

Eyes begin to roll as they all agree, "Well he will love that. That's just what he wants is to have it easy."

"But wait a minute," I interjected, "you just said that he loves ball more than anything. If that's true, then taking away what he loves will probably have the most profound effect on him."

I remember my mom telling me one day that if the dishes weren't done before she got home, then I wasn't going to soccer practice. "Yeah right," I thought. "They are paying great money for me to practice and taking time off work. What's going to happen, are we just going to sit at home?"

She wasn't kidding!! I missed practice and I will never forget how bad I felt. Let alone the face of the guy coaching as I walked up to the next session. "You hurt the team man." Boom! Like a dagger in the heart. You better believe them dishes have been spotless since!

You see, playing a sport is a privilege. In order to play on this team you have to meet certain standards.

Working at this company or in the office is a privilege. In order to work here there are certain standards that must be met.

You see, when most of us think of motivation we look toward extrinsic motivators, or things outside of the person that will kick them into gear.

Here are some traditional extrinsic motivators:

Wind sprints.
Increasing pay.
Opportunity for a day off.
Playing time.
Bonuses.
Physical punishment.
Sitting the bench.
Extra study hall.
Community service.
Yelling.
Throwing out threats.

Daniel Pink's research clearly shows that across the board these *can* work in the short-term, but long-term they are detrimental to growth and creativity.

"Carrots and sticks can achieve precisely the opposite of their intended aims. Mechanisms designed to increase motivation can dampen it. Tactics aimed at boosting creativity can reduce it. Programs to promote good deeds can make them disappear. Meanwhile, instead of restraining negative behavior, rewards and punishments can often set it loose—and give rise to cheating, addiction, and dangerously myopic thinking.....tangible rewards tend have a substantial negative effect on intrinsic motivation. When institutions focus on the short term and opt for controlling people's behavior, they do considerable long-term damage." (From, *Drive*, by Daniel Pink)

What we really need is to focus on how we can unearth people's intrinsic motivation.

I know you might be thinking, "But what if they just enjoy the time away? That doesn't help us!"

Two things. First, if they miss the rest of the day at practice or at work *they* will miss out on the information provided, and *they* will be the one responsible for catching up. If you miss a new inbound play that will probably affect whether or not you get to play in games. There can also be a boundary that if you don't practice, you don't play.

If you miss a meeting that shared significant information about one of your biggest clients, then that will significantly affect whether or not you are asked to work on the project.

If you miss a day in the office and don't call the family of the kid you are responsible for recruiting, your team may lose the opportunity to coach them in the future.

You've let yourself down. You've let your team and colleagues down. And you may even lose your position if the pattern continues.

The easiest and most simple way to create new behaviors is through enforcing clearly explained healthy boundaries with LOVE & RESPECT.

Secondly, if someone is *enjoying* their time away, then you have unearthed a bigger issue. I remember working with a program where the guy coaching asked one of his kids to step away for overstepping the boundary of focus. He was not paying attention as the information was shared with the team. "Nick, you've lost your opportunity to get better with the team today. Go sit on the bench."

Now, we do not want people to still be involved in practice. We want them to go home. But, it was interesting to see what happened. This young man had the time of his life while the rest of the team was training. It was simple from there. The guys coaching asked Nick if he *really* wanted to be playing ball on that team. He didn't. So the next day he left.

I am astounded that there are so many groups where close to 80% of the team's effort and energy is directed toward trying to pull one or two people along. They are acting as "energy vampires" as our friend Jon Gordon calls them.

Set the boundary.
Clearly communicate the boundary.
Enforce the boundaries with love and respect.
Watch the standards rise and new normals will be created.

Does it actually work though?

We set a boundary for timeliness in one of the teams I work with. The very next day three guys in the freshmen class showed up late to practice. The guy coaching came over and said, "What should I do?"

I said, "Well, what do you want to do?"

"I think I'm going to say 'It doesn't look like you are interested in getting better because you showed up late. You've overstepped the boundary. You've lost your opportunity to get better with the team today. Go home and we will see you tomorrow.' "

"Awesome," I said, "I'd like for you to drop the first part. We do not know *why* they are late. That is judgment, and it is irrelevant. They are late and that's all that matters."

So he walked right over to them, shared what he had prepared and then walked away like nothing had changed. When the guys came back the next day he treated them like nothing had happened and said, *"It's great to see you today. I can't wait to watch you work hard and get better."*

As it turned out, they *did* get pulled over by the police on the way. This guy's resolve not to judge them turned out to be something that significantly strengthened their relationship. All three guys texted him that night sincerely apologizing and they vowed to respect the boundaries moving forward. Since then, they have been on time for everything we do.

In one team, the lady coaching asked a girl to step out of practice because she was not giving the effort that they had set as a standard. The young lady stormed out of the gym. Later that night this is the text the lady coaching received:

> *"I just want to say sorry. I apologize. I was talking to myself like how I used to say 'I can't' and the whole time in boot camp I was saying 'I can.' I got in my head and wasn't listening to nobody. I'm sorry. I feel terrible. I was doing so well and now it just killed my confidence a little. I'll come back tomorrow hard. I understand that I've upset you really bad but I just wanted you to know that I'm sorry that I let you down. That's the very last thing I wanted to do."*

Response from the lady who coaches:

> *"I love you too much to allow you to make a choice like that and get away with it. You are going to make mistakes as we go but I trust that you will learn and grow from it. Come back tomorrow and get back to work."*

Kid's follow up:

"I'd be worried if you did let me get away with things like that. The last thing I want you to do is just let me get away with things. I want to get better and I know I have to mentally do that for myself. But I love you too coach. Just don't ever let me get away with anything. EVER!!! I am better than what I did today and today was my one mistake. I'm going to try better. I'll come back tomorrow motivated! Thank you for believing in me! I really appreciate it."

Response from the lady who coaches:

"I know you are better than that. Everyone is going to make mistakes but how you learn from it is what matters. I see you growing so much more this year and I'm excited to watch you!"

The fact of the matter is that many of us in leadership roles are spending way too much energy and time begging, bitching, pulling and prodding.

Sometimes it creates a change in the short-term, but long-term we are equipping our people with very poor strategies. *We might be reinforcing our need to be needed, but we are failing to allow consequences to teach. Moreover, we aren't giving our best energy to those on our team who are pursuing excellence.*

We do not want the people we mentor to enter into relationships, teams, or jobs where they have to have someone prodding them with a stick. We want to develop people who pursue excellence because they *want to.*

If you want to stop coaching effort and you actually want to *equip* and teach:

Don't bitch.
Don't beg.
Create and ENFORCE healthy boundaries and you will create
NEW Normals for your team.

TRAIN TO BE CLUTCH

- Make a list of the extrinsic motivators you find yourself using the most.

5 BIGGEST INHIBITORS TO YOUR GREATNESS

1.) **Busyness**: Sacrificing what is most important for what is most urgent.

2.) **Fixed Mindset**: Falling into the trap of trying to prove yourself instead of being focused on growth. Caring too much what it looks like and caring too little about what it really is.

3.) **Work Ethic**: Lack of understanding of hustle and grind. You need both.

4.) **Lack of Persistence**: Too caught up in instant gratification. Sacrificing who you want to become for what you want now.

5.) **Attitude**: Results are greatly tarnished if your attitude toward the work and others sucks.

CHAPTER 37

ANYTHING THAT HAPPENS IS AN OPPORTUNITY TO LEARN AND GROW

I TOLD MYSELF I would only go stand in line if I woke up naturally.

Sure enough I woke up at 4:52am without an alarm clock going off. So, I packed a light travel bag with some breakfast food, my computer, iPad, and notebook. I also brought a folding chair.

I expected to be there no longer than 2 or 3 hours, but I made myself this promise. **If you are going to do this, then this is about developing patience, *NOT* about getting the, *iPhone 6*.**

The system they had setup at the Manhattan Beach, CA *Apple store* was not very good. People were very frustrated after a couple hours. I did my best to focus on the opportunity to develop patience, because I knew it was something I could use A LOT more of in my life.

After over 6 hours of waiting in line, we were finally informed they were out of the phones. The people around me were furious to say the least. Every single person I saw felt like they had something taken from them. Their focus had been on getting an, *iPhone 6,* and when that was no longer a possibility, they felt robbed.

I was actually excited when they told me we could go home. I had lasted over 6 hours and that morning was an exercise in developing patience. It appeared I was the only person who felt that way though, as everyone else left with frustration and bitterness exploding from their eyes and mouths.

What we really believe often comes out when things don't go how we really want. **Is your commitment to the process and putting people's hearts first only a strategy you use when things are going well, or do you stick with it even when the results are not what you want?**

It's easy when we win and get what we want.

It's hard when we don't get the results we want.

As strange as it sounds, I was happy I didn't get the *iPhone 6* that day, because it's much easier to focus on developing the characteristics we want to embody *when* we are rewarded with what we want out of our circumstances.

Every experience, no matter how painful, hard, or bad, offers us an equal opportunity to gain something wonderful from it. The challenge is to be focused on developing the characteristics that actually matter instead of focusing on getting the win, the toy, or the desired result.

Often times it is in the most trying of circumstances where the strongest of character can be forged. It is not in the confines and safety of amazing circumstances where character is forged, it is during the exhausting, and painful times.

Don't sacrifice the stuff that matters at the altar of potentially winning. Character will take you further and sustain you more than results and achievement ever will.

TRAIN TO BE CLUTCH

- What is your iPhone 6? What do you need to let go of and focus on instead?
- Can you identify a time in your life where you were focused on the uncontrollable end result and when it didn't come you felt robbed?

CHAPTER 38

THE HABIT MYTH

YOU HAVE HEARD it.

Your group has heard it.

The problem is that it's NOT TRUE!

If you are anything like me, you have tried many times and succeeded in doing something for 21 days and THEN IT DOES NOT become a personal habit. The truth is that it depends on what type of habit you are trying to create, as well as what habits a person currently does or does not possess.

One study found:

"The time it took participants to reach 95% of their asymptote of automaticity ranged from 18 to 254 days; indicating considerable variation in how long it takes people to reach their limit of automaticity and highlighting that it can take a very long time."

The truth is that it takes a long time to form new habits, and if the habit is worthwhile then keep working at it until it becomes more automatically engrained in your daily routine. As we wrote about in the chapter, *A New Way To Operate*, the best way to engrain a new routine is by stacking the habit you want on top of a habit you already have.

Do not forget this:

Our brand is NOT
Do This Once And Be Clutch
Think And Be Clutch
Do This For 21 Days And Be Clutch

We are **Train** To Be Clutch.

Training is deliberate.
Training is consistent.
Training has no definite end.

We become who we train to be.

CHAPTER 39

STOP TRYING TO CHANGE PEOPLE

THERE'S A LOT to be said about sitting down regularly with people who have a lot of grey hair. My wife and I spent as much time as we could with a couple in Ireland who were in there sixties and some of the greatest wisdom we've received came out of those conversations over cups of tea.

Here's one little nugget that really stands out.

As Amy and I found out we were pregnant, Leslie encouraged us, *"Make sure that you don't make your child the focus. Focus on each other. If your marriage is great, your child will follow suit."*

Wow, not exactly what conventional wisdom would suggest. And it's not even something I had ever thought of. What a counter-cultural way of doing things!

I cannot even count the amount of times someone has come to me asking how they can help another person change. Whether it's someone who coaches, leads, plays or parents, I have realized that many of us have a deep desire to help people change.

Though people are wanting the right thing to say or the right team building exercise, my response is always the same: get better.

"But no, Jamie. How do I help *them*?"

"Simple, get better."

You see, I believe that we cannot change people, organizations, or teams, but we can always affect change. I've been around plenty of teammates and people in coaching who have tried to change the team through coercion. But usually those attempts created deeper divides in the team or created a short-term change that soon fizzled out.

We don't have control over results. We have control over what we commit to and who we are becoming. Too often people are pointing fingers at the things or people who need to change and that only takes our focus off of what we can do in the present. Instead of talking about people in your organization and the reasons they do what they do, you can:

- Read a great book.
- Watch helpful videos with beneficial content.
- Go over your highlight reel.
- Do extra physical preparation.
- Do something wonderful and unexpected for someone else.
- Write your What Went Well Journal.
- Practice sowing new beliefs.

All of these are within our control and will help us become the type of person that we want to become.

If we focus on improving our default mode of operation, we affect change in those around us. We create an environment of excellence as we model the belief that we are the people, flesh and blood, who have the most say about us on this earth. We change the environment that our team operates within. We change what they see, and in turn affect how they feel.

When we improve our default mode of operation we create an example that others can aspire to. And as they see the fruit in our lives, some, not all, will want to ask what has made that change.

One of the people I mentor who is in an assistant coaching role told me that she has carried our book around on every road trip. She has worked extremely hard at becoming the person she wants to be and it has become apparent to everyone around her that she has changed. So when one of the ladies asked what she was reading, it was no surprise that five other people leaned in on the conversation. Now, *Burn Your Goals*, is in the hands of a core group of the team. And who knows what can happen now!

If you are really wanting to see a change in your team, family, relationship, or organization, focus on getting better yourself.
Invest in becoming the type of person you want to be.
Focus on commitments.
Stop pointing the finger.
As Gandhi said, "Be the change that you want to see in the world."

And in doing that you will change the environment others operate in.
You'll change what they see.
You'll affect how they feel.

Any change that happens in the lives of others is a reflection of the change we have made in ourselves.

You only have so much time and energy every day, spend it on you getting better, because that is under your control.

TRAIN TO BE CLUTCH

- Read *The Question Behind The Question* by John Miller

CHAPTER 40

WILL YOU BE PROUD?

MY FRIEND HAD just recently found out his wife had been continuously cheating on him.

She told him she never loved him and had faked it the whole time they were married.

Yet this is what he told me:

"I hope to handle this situation in a way in which I can look back on it in 5 years and be proud of how I handled it."

WHAT?!!

Are you kidding me?!!

I'm not sure I've been through something that challenging, and yet here was this guy going through something horrific with an incredibly loving and powerful perspective.

No matter what you are currently going through, ask yourself, how can I handle this in a way that five years from now I can look back and be proud of how I handled it?

The other question you can ask is, who am I going to trust? Myself, or my Abba Father?

Those you lead might learn a lifetime of wisdom from your pain and perspective.

Recycle the pain.

Use it, don't let it use you.

TRAIN TO BE CLUTCH

- Watch: "Who Are You Going To Trust?" By Joshua Medcalf on Vimeo

CHAPTER 41

LINGUISTIC INTENTIONALITY

"Guys! I haven't been able to say a word to my team all day. Every time I went to say something I realized I was encouraging them in a way that promoted a fixed mindset. I've got to completely rethink everything I say to them."

We could feel the frustration in her voice, and I reminded her that we had warned that the path to transformational leadership would not be easy.

I suggested she get a notecard and one side of the card write out the DO NOT USE THESE WORDS & PHRASES. Then write out all the words and phrases she came across that are not the most beneficial ones to use. On the flip side of the card you write out USE THESE WORDS & PHRASES instead.

Some of the words on my 'DO NOT USE' list are as follows:

POSITIVE OR POSITIVITY

- The only exceptions being if I am describing a movement in a direction opposite of negative. I try to avoid the word *positive*, because it has a tendency of alienating people with a more cynical or negative mindset, AND I believe there are better words to use. The other exception is if I am specifically talking about Barbara Fredrickson's work on positivity and the Positivity Ratio.

TALENT

- This word is frequently used in ways that are destructive in my opinion. Sometimes we use the word to describe skills that are developed and other times we use it to describe something you cannot teach. Since we believe all skills, traits, and behaviors can be developed we suggest not using the word.
- We also believe the word pushes those you lead into the deadly and unproductive "fixed mindset" that Carol Dweck writes about in her book, *Mindset.* It leads some people to believe that you are either born with something or you're not. This causes many people to give up without trying.
- I ask people in leadership this question: "Who would you say are the *talented* ones in your group?" I follow up with, "Who do you have the hardest time leading and helping operate at their best?" Almost inevitably, the ones who are told they are *talented* don't believe they have to work hard.
- A more beneficial word is "skill."

NICE SHOT

- Any word or phrase that is praising the outcome or result would probably be better off avoided. This type of praise once again pushes people towards a fixed mindset.
- We encourage people to praise growth and process. For example, "great form," "I loved how you made sure you got your feet set on that one," "I know you worked really hard on that project, it was very quality work," "I loved how committed you were on that one."

Linguistic intentionality is all about asking the question, "Is this the most *beneficial* word or phrase I can use?

Once again, it is dirty hard work to rewire our brains in this manner, but it is worth it. The woman we referred to at the beginning of the chapter helped her team go on a winning frenzy never before seen in the program. Hard work pays off.

TRAIN TO BE CLUTCH

- What are some of your most used phrases or words? If you can't think for sure, as a co-worker, spouse or one of the people you lead?
- Does each phrase lead people towards a growth or fixed mindset?
- Sometimes, talking less actually achieves more. This lady also reduced her amount of communication by 50%.
- Read, *Wooden On Leadership* by John Wooden
- Read, *The Talent Code* by Daniel Coyle
- Read, *Talent Is Overrated* by Geoff Colvin

CHAPTER 42

THE POWER OF EXAMPLE

I WAS FEELING great leading up to our first game. I felt prepared physically and mentally. I loved the guy who was playing next to me. And I was really looking forward to the stories and path that would unfold over the next 12 weeks.

Then we lost 1-0.....

And began the start of a season that on paper looked absolutely miserable! But for me, and for a few others, it was a season of transformation.

I remember the first road trip clearly. We were sitting at the check in counter at Denver International Airport excited for a 4-day trip. Everyone had their Beats by Dre headphones on and we were waiting for someone to bust out the playing cards for a game of Deuce Deuce.

The guy sitting next to me wanted to talk, I could feel it, but I had already made the commitment to read Geoff Colvin's book, *Talent Is Overrated*, on that trip. **Though I *felt* like playing cards and chilling, I knew that I wanted to read and I would be better off to live by my principles rather than my feelings.**

On that first trip I was the *ONLY* guy with a book in hand.

The second trip started out the same. I walked up to a rowdy card game and tons of laughter, but this time Daniel Pink's book, *Drive*, was my travel companion. I sat down on the plane with book in hand and my buddy Mejia sat down next to me. Sure enough he pops out a book, Victor Frankl's *Man's Search For Meaning*. It started a conversation and friendship that we still hold to this day.

Next to him was a fella named Acchio, at least that sounds like what people call him. Though broken up on the plane because of seating, Deuce Deuce remained the focal point for our team passing cards between seats and across the aisle. As Mejia and I were reading and chatting intermittently, Acchio told the fellas he was stepping out of the game.

Sure enough, he pulled out a book his coach asked the team to read. You could tell he wanted to be somewhere else, but something was pulling him toward the book....

What was it?

You see in every context there is a social norm. On our team it was chilling and playing Deuce Deuce. When someone steps out of the norm and tries to take it in a different direction, there is always friction and resistance.

- Maybe the norm is to complain about your leadership team at the water cooler or at happy hour.
- Maybe the norm is to talk about the people coaching behind their back in the locker room.
- Maybe the norm is to cut people down with "innocent" jokes. *There is power of life and death in the tongue.
- Maybe the norm is to only go half speed during fitness so no one looks bad.
- Maybe the norm is to focus on performance rather than transformation.
- Maybe the norm is to focus on profit rather than people.

But by staying committed to a particular process, you can actually start to change the norm for those around you.

While we were at Vanderbilt the norm was to party at night on the weekends. Joshua and I decided that we wanted to get better at soccer and actually trained from 10 pm to 1 am one night almost every weekend. There was resistance, but slowly people wanted to join us. It got to the point that we said, "No, you can't play with us. But you can go to the other end of the field and train if you want to."

When we begin creating a new normal for ourselves, we challenge the social norms. And as we all know, "the rising tide floats all the boats." In other words, you inevitably raise the standard of the social norm. You create *NEW NORMALS*.

Fast forward to week 10 and I am sitting on the plane coming home from Vegas. I look around and there are 4 people holding the number 1 book we recommend, *Mindset*, by Carol Dweck. 3 people are reading our first book, *Burn Your Goals*. And every time someone asked me a question, you could see at least 5 other people lean in to glean what they could from the conversation.

What I have seen this season only confirmed what I already knew: *When we work on creating a new normal, we create an environment where change in others is possible.*

It may take some time......a *REALLY* long time!

My life was forever changed by a guy named Tim Lonergan. Joshua's life was greatly impacted as well. For 3 years he loved Jesus and loved people like I had never seen before. He never beat me over the head about the Bible or how far my life was from what it taught. In fact, he never even told any of us on the team that he was a Christian. *He lived a life of love.*

People literally acted completely different in front of him, and he never asked anyone to. People wouldn't cuss, or would apologize for cussing around him. They would change the topics of conversation, because when they were around him they felt different.

And when my life took an unexpected turn I asked myself a simple question:

Who do I want to be?

The answer was clear. I wanted to be like Tim and I knew Tim loved Jesus. It took 3 years for that change to happen, but everything you read comes from his investment in committing to something outside the social norm.

Instead of trying to push and prod your teammates, those you lead on your team, children, spouse, or friends, ***focus on changing YOU***. It's the only thing that is controllable. Often when we stop focusing on changing others and just focus on all our areas for personal growth we end up changing the world around us as a by-product.

TRAIN TO BE CLUTCH

- What are you committed to doing over the next 2 weeks that will help you raise your default mode of operation?
- We don't have to be perfect, but we have to be committed.
- One guy who coaches decided to read during his lunch break instead of talking with others. Within two weeks he finished a book.
- If we took back thirty minutes of every day for a whole year, we would have 182.5 hours to direct toward something that would make a difference.

CHAPTER 43

GIVE VS GET

IT'S AMAZING WHAT happens when you shift from what you can get to what you can give.

Lots of people talk about it. Very few people in leadership *truly* model it.

TRAIN TO BE CLUTCH

- Watch Michael Jr.'s 3 minute video "Be The Punchline" on YouTube. His shift is the most incredible example we could find. His "big break" came when he shifted from trying to *get* laughs from his audiences, to *giving* them an opportunity to laugh.

CHAPTER 44

THIS IS *YOUR* LIFE. ARE YOU WHO *YOU* WANT TO BE?

I WANT YOU to take a second and think of somebody.

Not just anybody. I want you to think of a person who you know. A person in whom you see so much potential. You see they have so much to give and they aren't even coming close to tapping into what's possible.

If they would only wake up, and choose to use what they have, fan it into flame, there is no telling what kind of influence they could have.

You got that person in mind?

Okay, chances are you'll come into contact with that person today. But *there is an even greater chance* **you are that person** *someone else is thinking about.*

I remember sitting in the car with Joshua driving through Santa Monica, California 3 years ago when he hit me in the chest with these words:

"Are you going to tell your kids to chase their dreams? If so, you better have chased yours."

And I did. And I haven't stopped since. It's been a crazy journey. It's been excruciatingly trying physically, spiritually, and emotionally.

Walking onto a professional soccer team in Major League Soccer was one of the loneliest experiences of my life.

Getting match fit after being injured for 2 years was unbelievably painful and tough.

Receiving only 3 constructive comments in 5 months from the people coaching that team made me wonder if God really loved me and called me to this.

Even now as I share stories with multitudes of people, it terrifies me every day.

But I know that the only true risk for me is to settle and not take risks at all. If I want to become what I'm created to be I am responsible for climbing the mountains and chasing the lions in my life.

But what about you?

What's that dream that's still residing in your soul? What's the passion you had as a kid that has been suppressed by you doing what you "should be doing?"

What can you begin to do to close the gap between who you are and who you want to become?

Remember: *Dream BIG, think small.*
Do the best you can, with what you have, right where you are.

What can you begin to do to close the gap between where you are and where you want to be?

Maybe that's as simple as doodling an image on a scrap piece of paper.

Maybe it's as simple as doing a physical workout.

Maybe it's buying a book that you've always wanted to read.

Maybe it's selling everything you own and moving to a 3rd world country to serve?

Maybe it is writing an article a week about the 3 most important lessons you learned that week in your position as a human being who happens to be a businessman, businesswoman, coach, mom, player, lawyer, architect, photographer, athletic director, or any other profession.

Whatever it is, I would encourage you to simply make a start. **The inconvenient truth is that if you don't start today, it will ALWAYS be more challenging to start tomorrow.**

What is your dream?
What is your passion?
What is the smallest vision of that dream that you can begin today?

Every day we have the ability to point fingers at others and their unwillingness to close the gap. But when we point the finger at others we always have 3 fingers pointing back at us.

It's simple:
This is your life.
Are you who you want to be?

TRAIN TO BE CLUTCH

- Listen to "This Is Your Life" by the band Switchfoot
- Read *In A Pit With A Lion On A Snowy Day* by Mark Batterson

CHAPTER 45

"YOU CAN'T WIN LIKE THAT......CAN YOU?"

"THERE IS A lot more to life than football. It's not life or death."

That is a phrase I'm not sure a lot of people involved in big money football are used to hearing, or more likely, not used to seeing practically lived out.

- Family dinners during the season every Sunday evening.
- Team dinners in the middle of every week.
- As much golf as possible in the off-season.
- Dinner with the wife almost every night.
- Bodysurfing when the weather cooperates.

None of these sound like the habits of those coaching at the highest levels of BCS football. Yet, they are the habits and words of a man who won a Heisman trophy at Florida, won a national championship while coaching at Florida, won the last conference championship for Duke football, and has the most wins of anyone in coaching at Florida and South Carolina.

Steve Spurrier's ideals on enjoyment and family are an enigma in this world, but I believe they are a great example for anyone in leadership. He has put first things first in his life, and he has still been successful, some might even say he has been *wildly* successful in his career.

*Be careful you don't sacrifice everything that is ACTUALLY important in your life at the altar of **potentially** winning.*

TRAIN TO BE CLUTCH

- What are your priorities in life?
  1.)
  2.)
  3.)
  4.)
  5.)
- Does the way you use your time reflect those priorities? If not, you will most likely experience a lot of internal frustration.
- What has *not* putting first things first in your life cost you?
- What could it cost you in the future if you don't make immediate changes?
- Watch the YouTube video: *How To Make Work-Life Balance Work* by Nigel Marsh
- Agreement with yourself: (I would actually write this out and sign it if I were you.)

I_____ commit to doing _____

_____ every week, and cutting out _____

every week in order to create better balance and start putting first

things first in my life.

Signed: _____Date: _____

- Watch the YouTube video: *How To Make Work-Life Balance Work* by
  Nigel Marsh

CHAPTER 46

UP UNTIL NOW

"THAT'S GREAT JAMIE. I think a lot of what you presented this week is awesome, but I don't know that the girls are going to respond to it the way you think they will."

These are the words from a lady who coaches at the Division 1 level. I get it, many of you may be thinking, *"Yeah, in an ideal world this would be an awesome way to lead, coach, and parent, BUT you don't know my kids, my employees, or my team. They don't show signs of being able to operate with autonomy. When I give them an inch, they take a mile."*

I get it.

My response to her and to you is simple:

Have you ever operated the way we have laid out for at least 6 months?

I was talking with a girl who plays college golf and she was telling me all the things that she has been accustomed to doing in the past. For the last 2 years she has bogeyed number seventeen and eighteen, no matter what course she played. She was frustrated and really desperate for change.

I smiled. Why, did I smile? Because that was in the past.

"You're right," I said, "that stuff has happened. And up until now, you, by your own admission, have played out of fear, trained minimal hours, been very unfocused in your practice, have had less than beneficial self-talk, negatively visualized, and have compared yourself to everyone around you.

"Up until now, that is how you have operated, and the results have been similar. But everything changes when we consistently change our now."

You see, what I have found is that most of us look at how we have operated and the results we have had in the past and try to move forward like we are driving in the rearview mirror. We expect the same things to happen. Sure, we don't say that, but that is how our beliefs are shaped: from our experience in the past and what we believe to be true about the future.

Everything changes when we change our now. It just may not happen over night. You don't gain 100 pounds in a month, and you don't lose 100 pounds in a month either.

So I said to the lady who coaches, "If you are spending time working on visualizing your highlight reel, using beneficial self-talk, reading wisdom, sowing new beliefs, practicing constructive body language and seeking out challenges for at least 3-6 months, then we should not expect the same results."

Have you ever operated like this? If the answer is no, then you have no idea how things could change in the future. You need to believe that your mode of operation and results will not be the same in the future.

Here is a phrase I would encourage you to use:

Up until now_____. BUT NOW, _____.

For me, up until the last year, I had lived out of fear and a scarcity mindset. BUT NOW, I choose to operate out of love and abundance. This has created 'new normals' in my life, my business, and for my family.

What could your 'BUT NOW' statements be? Here are some examples from a friend who coaches at the Division 1 level, and is working hard to become transformational.

Up until now, I have worried about what others think of me in coaching and parenting. ***BUT NOW,*** I make decisions out of love and with conviction.

Up until now, when I walk into a room I have been fearful of how others are judging me. ***BUT NOW,*** I choose to remember that I am no longer judged and am free to love others.

Up until now, I have worried about sounding dumb and whether or not someone wants to talk to me on the phone. ***BUT NOW,*** I choose to speak with confidence and love.

Up until now, I have tried to please everyone in my decisions so that I don't hurt feelings. ***BUT NOW,*** I make decisions drawing on wisdom and in confidence believing that the decisions are in everyone's best interest.

Up until now, I have felt bad delegating tasks to other people. ***BUT NOW,*** I choose to utilize the gifts that those around me have while respecting their boundaries.

Up until now, I have worried about saying hard things to help people move forward. ***BUT NOW,*** I choose to touch on real issues because I love them too much to let them stay where they are.

Up until now, I have worried that I ask God for too much. **BUT NOW** I choose to engage with my Father as often as I can.

Up until now, I have been waiting for the wheels to come off of anything that is going well. **BUT NOW** I choose to enjoy and focus on being at my best in the present knowing that I cannot control the future.

Up until now, my team's mistakes have consumed my energy and focus. **BUT NOW** I choose to see the things that they are doing well and fan those into flames.

Up until now, I have been afraid of failing and have chosen to play it safe. **BUT NOW** I choose to take on tough challenges that put me outside my comfort zone.

Up until now, I have had no boundaries and some in my family have suffered as I devoted attention to my team, business, and certain individuals. **BUT NOW** I am giving my best to those I love and decisively say no to things outside of my core commitments and mission for my life.

Up until now, I have not been very prayerful and have not devoted my life entirely to Christ. **BUT NOW** I choose to trust in Him and lean not on my own understanding.

These are not easy or comfortable changes. Sowing these beliefs and coupling them with action is a step of great faith.

We understand that what we present is countercultural. It does take courage to step out. But it's exactly what we are asking of those

JOSHUA MEDCALF & JAMIE GILBERT

we parent, lead, and coach. We want them to do what they haven't done so that they can become who they have never been. We want them to try what they have never tried so that they can go where they have never gone.

All of this requires faith.

Dr. Martin Luther King Jr. said, "Faith is taking a step when you cannot see the entire staircase."

TRAIN TO BE CLUTCH

- Write out 5 beliefs you hold about yourself or ways that you operate that you would like to change.
- Write out what you would like to believe or how you would like to operate instead.
- Create 5 of your own Up Until Now statements using the information above and the structure below:

Up until now_____. BUT NOW, _____.

CHAPTER 47

WHAT DO YOU PLAN TO NEGLECT?

THE ONLY COMMON denominator for everyone in the world is time. From the person currently living on the streets to people performing at the top levels in music, sports, and business. **Everyone on this earth has 86,400 seconds in a day. The difference between most of us is how we use that time and how faithful we are with what we have.**

It's easy to complain about the talent you don't have, the genes you wish you had, and the opportunities and resources of the lucky ones. It is ridiculously hard to be faithful with what you DO have and become the best you can be using what you have.

Almost every person I talk to who coaches, runs a business, parents a child, or plays a sport tells me the same thing: *I don't have enough time to read.*

I was working with a group that plays D-1 sports and I was talking about the benefits of reading. Their coach stopped me in the middle of the workshop and said,

"I get the importance of reading. I have a hard time getting through books. What can you do for a guy like me? Are there cliff's notes or something?"

Turning toward him and in front of his whole team I said, "If I was going to pay you $10,000 to read Carol Dweck's *Mindset* by tomorrow night would you do it?"

"Of course!" he said sharply.

"Exactly! You do what you *value*!"

It's simple, we make time for what we value. Now, as someone who is married, has a child, trains, and works, I understand that there are plenty of things that can cause us to lose focus during a day.

Some things *necessitate* our attention, but to other things we *donate* our attention.

When my son fell off the couch and couldn't walk, that necessitated my attention.
When someone reaches out to me on twitter, I donate my attention.

So here is what I have found to be very helpful. Most mornings, or even the night before, I sit down and write out things that I plan to neglect during the day.

I took this idea from John Maxwell who taught me that self-control is a spiritual discipline that we all can operate in, but we have to choose to do so. Planning neglect is one of the most helpful tools to grow in that area.

As I am writing this part of the book, I am constantly seeing messages pop up in my inbox with all sorts of offers for extra-early deals for black Friday.

We just moved into a new apartment and don't have a dinner table. Honestly, we are eating off a Little-Tike table. The desire to peruse IKEA, American Furniture, and Craigslist is astounding.

And it's snowing outside in Denver and I really really *really* want to go out on my new snowboard.

None of these things *necessitate* my attention. There is nothing wrong with any of these things. I have the money to buy a table, I can drive 45 minutes to the mountains and I can do some Christmas shopping if I want to. But, I know that these things are not going to help me finish something that could impact and influence countless lives across the world.

I don't *have* to. I *choose* to. And when I am done writing I will go out there and enjoy the snow knowing that I have put first things first.

I know that people in leadership feel like they *have* to do certain things:

I *have* to respond to my colleagues' emails.

I *have* to call this person we are recruiting and their family.

I *have* to stay and talk to this person who coaches one of the kids we are recruiting.

I *have* to respond to this person studying in college who is asking for my time.

So what happens is that we don't create healthy boundaries. We don't devote ourselves to the meat of our work. And often, we spend too much of our time on the distractions of being busy instead of sitting down and making the time to do the hard work.

It is easy to respond, it is hard to do the real work.

What could happen if you planned to say no to certain people, tasks, or offers? One basketball staff has decided to insert in their emails the status of when the email needs to actually be dealt with:

"Question about the Denver trip (Not needed til Friday)"

They also know that each person on staff has the ability to say, "Unless this is an emergency, I am working on _____ for the next 20 minutes. Can we talk then?" and no one is allowed to get upset.

Much has been written about the importance of the psychological *flow* state and how challenging it is to get into it given the current world of distractions we live in, so we have to be extremely diligent about carving out that space. This is why Joshua never has his phone on ringer or vibrate. He doesn't want his flow to be interrupted, so he keeps it on silent and then looks at his phone periodically.

Try this. Donald Miller asks a fantastic question that I'd like you to ponder.

If you could do today all over again, what would you do differently?

I love that! If you have a hard time answering that question forwardly, think about yesterday, the last month, or the last season. How would you have used your time differently?

- Would you have taken the bait to engage in that argument?
- Would you have responded to some of the emails you chose?
- Would you have spent less time on *Pinterest*?
- Would you have spent more time in gratefulness prayer and meditation?
- Would you have spent more time exercising and eating healthier?
- Would you have said something specific and sincere to your significant other?

- Would you have made more time for prayer and reading God's Word?
- Would you have made more time for reading?

If we can answer that question looking back, it gives us a good barometer for looking at all the things that are begging for our time today and that will beg for our time in the future.

The big thing is that most of us feel like we are out of control. We often feel that we are not the ones on this earth that have the most to say about our lives. But when we put tangible action on exercising self-control, we feel empowered and we are way more productive and focused.

Warren Buffet has an exercise he used that is helpful in defining some of the things we should avoid at all costs. He would write out his top 25 goals. Again we don't believe in goals but that is the language he uses. He would then narrow it down to his top 5 goals. The other 20 that didn't make the cut became his AVOID AT ALL COSTS list.

It is easy to fall prey to the constant distractions and time sucks we have on our lives. I find it interesting that many of the people who make television shows and movies, rarely ever watch TV. There is nothing inherently wrong with TV, but I do find that interesting. There will always be people and distractions pulling for our attention, but our responsibility is to know where and how to put *first things first* in our lives.

TRAIN TO BE CLUTCH

- We do what we value.
- Some things *necessitate* our attention. To other things we *donate* our attention.
- Some people want our time. Other people need our time.
- If you could do today over, what would be different?

- The greatest predictor of future success is the ability to delay instant gratification.
- What do you plan to neglect today?
- "God has not given us a spirit of fear, but one of power, love, and **self-control**" (*ESV* 2 Timothy 1:7)

CHAPTER 48

PERFECTIONISM CRIPPLES MORE PEOPLE THAN IT HELPS

OUR FIRST BOOK, Burn Your Goals, has at least 50 typos and all sorts of grammatical issues. Many people who read the final drafts said, "You CANNOT publish this."

We did it anyway, and it is changing the way many people look at sport psychology around the world and has had a greater impact than we ever could have imagined. We didn't and don't try to write with typos and grammatical issues, but they happen.

The key was, we didn't let it stop us or slow us down. Too many people use the excuse of being a perfectionist to stop them from providing value to the world that someone desperately needs in *that* moment, and not a moment later.

Give your VERY VERY best.

Pursue excellence.

But don't cripple yourself with the illusion of perfection.

TRAIN TO BE CLUTCH

- Read, *The Lean Startup,* by Eric Ries
- Read, *Steal Like An Artist,* by Austin Kleon

CHAPTER 49

DESPERATION IS NOT A GOOD LOOK ON YOU

"YA, SHE COMMITTED to us," he said excitedly!

Not overly joyful like hearing a "YES" from your high school crush, but like it was never a doubt in his mind and things would be great either way.

"So what did you say to her?" I asked.

He said he had been following her intently all over the world in the recruiting process and had numerous conversations. She was really the only person he wanted and was looking at heavily. You would think with all of that time, travel, and energy invested he would be *desperate* to get her there and would have had to promise her the world.

"It's simple Jamie, I told her that she is going to be fantastic here, but the program is going to do cool things with or without her."

WHAT?!!

This was a far cry from what I hear from many people responsible for recruiting. This was a girl was one of the top recruits in the world, and she just turned down many offers to top 20 schools to choose *HIS* school. Yet, he acted as if it was *supposed* to happen.

Too often there is such desperation to sign or hire a particular person who we **think** will take the group to another level that we offer them the world. But how we come off most of the time is really *desperate.*

When we have that insatiable desire we get needy and we are like that person in a relationship who actually ends up driving the other person away because of their desperation and neediness.

One of my favorite people in leadership tells people regularly that his organization is too hard for most people who show interest. His reasoning: "I want people who are in love with the process of becoming great. And that process is dirty and hard."

At *Train To Be CLUTCH* we often do our best to talk people out of our mentorship program and bringing us out to speak. We want to make sure they realize it is a very serious time and financial investment and we want to make sure it is a really good fit. Sometimes it is a great fit, but many times it is not. We want to do our best to make sure we figure that out as early as possible *BEFORE* we start working with someone.

I wonder what it would look like if you actually started telling people the truth and weren't so dependent upon them?

Imagine what it would look like if you told a person, "You know what, we would love to have you here, but honestly it seems like A, B, and C would be a better fit for you considering what you are really passionate about. Do you know them personally? Here is their contact info, and I am going to call them and recommend you to them."

If you coach, resists the urge to laugh out loud after reading that, because people rarely trust you in the recruiting process. And why should they? They have heard all about the Dr. Jekyll and Mr. Hyde transformation during the recruiting process.

Imagine how much trust you would build, *not* just with that individual kid, but ALL around the country if that became your dominant way of recruiting. Stories like these would quickly become like the infamous story of *Nordstrom's* clothing store giving a refund for a car tire.

One of my mentors, Russ Pillar, taught me...

"Truth + Trust + Transparency = Transformation"

It wasn't until I became confident in who I was that I finally started to attract the type of women I was interested in dating. When I was needy and desperate I repelled the type of people I was interested in seriously dating. Don't be that person....

Stop begging and pleading for people to join your mission.

Do cool stuff.

Put first things first.

Be confident in your mission.

You just might start *attracting* people you only dreamed of having on your team.

CHAPTER 50

WHAT GETS YOUR ATTENTION IS WHAT YOU GET MORE OF

WHAT GETS YOUR attention? What gets your praise?

"Well done out there guys! You fought hard, and you deserved to win!"

I couldn't help but wonder if the ball had bounced the other way had ALL that effort been categorized as "just not good enough" or "sloppy or lazy".

People know what we value from what we give attention to and what we praise.

Do we praise the process regardless of results, or do those we lead know the process is only valuable when we use it to manipulate the result we wanted?

Do we give our attention to the one with the MOST URGENT drama or do we not engage and focus our energy on where we think it is most beneficial, NOT where it is most wanted?

Those we lead quickly recognize what we value from what we praise and what gets our attention.

Praise growth and the process, instead of results.

Give your best energy to areas you think are most beneficial and most important, not necessarily most pressing.

TRAIN TO BE CLUTCH

- Watch "<u>Carol Dweck- A Study On Praise</u>" on YouTube

CHAPTER 51

WHERE DO YOU FIND YOUR IDENTITY?

WHO WOULD YOU *BE* if everything you *DO* was taken away from you?

It's a very slippery slope to find your identity in what you do because in the climate of today's culture your job can be lost in a split second. You could be in a serious accident that leaves you unable to *do* the thing in which you find your identity. A loved one could be taken from you and leave you with a completely different set of circumstances.

Who would you be then?

Where do you find your identity?

I teach this stuff and this is one of the hardest things for me at times. It is so easy for me to get caught up in the results I get from working with people. It is so easy to get lost in the retweets about our books and workshops. It is so easy to get wrapped up in what I do.

I constantly have to remind myself that my value comes from who I am, NOT from what I do. It is easy to feel like our value is so much greater when our teams win, when we make a lot of money, when we experience great success in business. It is just as easy to be defeated and depressed when our teams aren't winning, when our businesses are failing, and when it feels like we suck at *everything*!

The TRUTH is, our value is constant, it's priceless, never going up or down based off results or our performance. Our value comes from who we are, NOT from what we do.

You are more than a mom.
You are more than a dad.
You are more than a coach.
You are more than a CEO.
You are more than a fast food worker.
You are more than an athlete.

We work very hard to always write and say, a **PERSON**, who does or serves as a _____. We do this very intentionally because when your identity gets wrapped up in what you do, it clouds every decision you make. It is easy to see some of the reasons that a person would make very compromising decisions when their identity comes from what they do.

For me personally, the only thing I want my identity to be found in is being a child of God. I believe that is something that I can never lose, and it can never be taken away from you or me. You may not believe that, and you don't have to agree with me. But I do challenge you to find your identity in something that cannot be stripped away in a moments notice.

CHAPTER 52

A SPECIFIC AND SINCERE COMPLIMENT

ANSON DORRANCE TAUGHT me a very valuable lesson. He taught me that a specific and sincere compliment can change the entire trajectory of a person's life. He doesn't even know he taught me this, but he will after he reads this. He didn't share this lesson with me. He showed me.

It probably took him less than a minute to type this email to me, "Joshua, your workshop was EXCELLENT! I loved your story, your content, and your delivery." It may have not meant a lot to him at the time, but it meant the world to me. It has fueled me for the last 3 years and it has changed not only the trajectory of my life, but the lives of those I have had the privilege of impacting.

We don't need 21 national championship titles to impact someone's life with a specific and sincere compliment. I've had the pleasure of meeting a lot of people around the world, but one of my favorite people by far is Kelia Moniz. She has a presence unlike anything I have ever seen. When she walks into a room everyone can feel her presence. She is one of the sweetest and kindest people I know.

The first time I met her we were standing outside of Cheesecake Factory after church and I asked her, "Where does your swagger come from?" She told me it came from God. I was intrigued, and that was pretty much the end of the conversation as we went separate ways.

Our mutual friend, Ryan, told me she had just won a world championship for surfing. Later that night I sent her a tweet encouraging her and telling her about the impact her presence has on people. I gave her a specific and sincere compliment. I also sent her some tools and told her I would love to sit down with her if she ever had the time.

The next afternoon we sat down at a street side pizza shop in Westwood, California, and I poured into her life. I told her a lot of stories and encouraged her with lots of specific and sincere compliments. On multiple occasions tears welled up in her eyes and I could see her fighting to keep them from flowing down her face.

I was shocked! Here is a girl who has reached the pinnacle of her sport, who is surrounded by some of the most powerful people in the world on a daily basis, yet my words were clearly moving her in powerful ways.

There is power of life and death in our words. Use them wisely. Sometimes it is the person we would never guess needs it who could benefit the most from a specific and sincere compliment. Oftentimes it is the very thing we think someone knows they bring to the table that we actually need to compliment. I've personally experienced it, and I've seen the impact on hundreds of people.

Write a note.
Send a text.
Leave a voicemail.

Make sure you don't ever miss an opportunity to give a specific and sincere compliment.

When we hold positions of leadership our words and actions are multiplied, so make sure you are using your words in ways you want them to be multiplied.

CHAPTER 53

OUR THOUGHTS ON FILM

WE ARE FIRM believers in using film only as a means of showing what went well and perfect film, of people who play high level college or professionally, as a means of teaching. We believe we wrap muscle memory by watching things; therefore, we want as many images of the skill or task being done well going through our heads as possible.

For me personally, I almost never watch film of a speaking engagement without having someone in my inner circle watch it first and tell me whether it is highlight film or not. If it is not highlight film, then there is no need for me to watch it. I only want to see myself at my very best, so that when I go on stage next time those are the images I have in my mind and I hopefully go out and replicate what I am seeing in my head.

The only caveat for using "negative" film is if someone does not believe they are doing something that they *are* doing. For example, in basketball if a person travels before they put the ball on the ground. Or if a person who plays golf believes they are swinging on a plane inside-out but they are actually on a plane going outside-in. I would first try and put them in the correct position multiple times, and show them on film or in demonstration the correct way of doing it, and if they are adamant that they are doing it the correct way, even when they are not, THEN I would show them ONE time on film how they are actually doing it.

Bear Bryant coached at Alabama and went down in history as one of the best of all time, and he apparently never used negative film either.

I have seen some people be able to constructively teach through film in a group setting, but I have seen many more examples where film becomes a torture session where people are made to feel shame. Shame has been shown to create a trauma on the brain, and is not optimal for peak performance. Shame might get a "positive" response out of some, but it in no way is tapping into a person's greatest potential.

Studying highlight film of yourself or of someone else who you want to emulate is a daily exercise we *HIGHLY* recommend. Our clients who take studying highlight reels and purposeful visualization the most serious are the ones we see thriving in their discipline.

TRAIN TO BE CLUTCH

- What person/people do you want to emulate in your discipline? Can you find clips of them on YouTube?
- If not, what can you remember them doing? Write out a list of memories you have of them operating the way you want to operate. Spend 20 seconds reliving each memory 3 times a week.
- When is a time you were at your very best? Try and relive that moment every day for one or 2 minutes see yourself at your very best, overcoming obstacles, and operating full of confidence.

WHAT DOES YOUR FACE SAY?

I WAS SITTING in a hotel getting ready to return home from a week of travel with a few teams I was working with and found myself watching one of those shows on the discovery channel. I think it was something like *Yukon Men.* I was listening to these guys talk about something that was happening in their town and knowing what I know about Carol Dweck's Fixed Mindset vs. Growth Mindset I was shocked to hear the prevalence of their fixed mindset.

I know, I judged them. I'm not proud of it. But I did.

What was equally as bad was what I noticed seconds later. There was a mirror that was just behind the TV and for whatever reason, I looked up and saw my facial expression. It was the most judgmental expression a human being could make!

As one who diligently trains intentional body language, it was interesting to see how easily my feelings get portrayed through my facial expression.

I have noticed this throughout my playing career as well. When I see a guy who is struggling to breathe and looks desperate, I know I have him beat. Likewise, when my opponent has that look of enjoying being absolutely tired, I get defeated! *"What does he know that I don't? And what is he taking!?!"*

One of the ladies I get to train coaches at the Division 1 level. She had told me that she gets really frustrated when her girls make silly mistakes. We all do. Any parent who has gone through potty train-ing can agree that it's ridiculous and frustrating. Unless you are one of those parents whose kid went on the potty the first time, in which case, God bless you!

I mean the toilet is right there. You don't like the pee running down your leg. And you don't like mommy and daddy staring at you from 3 feet away all day long!

It's simple: USE THE TOILET!!!!

So, I asked her if she thought she exuded her frustration in visible ways to her team. She agreed that her body language was either to throw her head back as to look at the heavens and say "Why God WHY!?!" Other times she would put her head down almost in shame of what she saw. So we started to work on that.

I asked her to go somewhere in the house where she would be alone and had access to a mirror. For 20 seconds I wanted her to stand in front of the mirror, close her eyes, and think about one of those silly mistakes happening. She could even relive one from the recent past. I wanted her to really try to put herself in the mo-ment. Once she was there and could feel it, she had to open her eyes quickly.

"So what did you find out?" I asked on our next call.

"I was appalled!" she said, "I looked like such a witch!"

Awesome! You see, we show a lot of how we feel by our facial expres-sion. If we are not intentional with the faces we make, we could be tear-ing someone down without ever uttering a word.

Try it yourself. See what it looks like when:

- Your staff has still not made the call you asked them to make.
- When your child unintentionally hits you in the face with play dough.
- When your team is trailing in a game and is lacking confidence.
- When you have received the news in front of your team that your biggest client has pulled out.
- When your spouse has returned home late from work without letting you know.
- When your child is struggling to sleep in the middle of the night.

If it's not the most beneficial expression, then use the same exercise to practice a more beneficial look.

We are great at coaching body language in our team, and we hold very high standards for how they carry themselves. But oftentimes we need to take a hard look in the mirror at what our own body language is communicating.

When it all hits the fan, those you lead are looking to you to see how you react.

Are you calm and confident? Or do you have a look of defeat, frustration, and anger?

Can they look to you for strength and direction? Or do they avoid eye contact because they know you are mad at them?

In the heat of the moment, you are either giving strength to your team, or you are sucking it out of them. Make sure you have trained for those moments, because we all know they are going to be extremely challenging.

Transformational leadership is about being the Rock of Gibraltar for your team even when you don't feel like it.

CHAPTER 55

PRINCIPLES VS. FEELINGS

HE WAS PUMPED.

He was shocked.

He was torn.

But he knew he had to make a decision.

One of my good friends who gets to coach at the Division 1 level had called me for advice as he had just received a pretty interesting phone call. It was the guy serving as the Athletic Director at a big name school who was offering my friend the head-coaching job.

Not only was it a big time school, it was my friend's dream school and was very close to his hometown and family. It brought all the perks of upgraded facilities, significant funding, and an increase in pay north of two hundred thousand.

What was wrong? Well, he was torn. On one hand, he thought this might be one of those lions that Mark Batterson talks about chasing in his book, *In A Pit With A Lion On A Snowy Day*. "Jamie, maybe this is one of those opportunities that scares me but God wants me to chase it."

"Maybe so," I said.

His heart was in one place and his head in another. He knew that the job would come with certain challenges that could be very difficult, but he knew he could take them head on.

To me, it really wasn't a matter of which one looked more appealing. So I asked him about his current team and staff and he began talking about them with a sincere depth of love and care. And then it surfaced:

"You know Jamie, in every recruiting visit I always tell the parents and girls that I am not going to up and leave because of an opportunity for more money at a big name school."

I can clearly remember my eyebrows rising when I heard that as I was in the *Golfsmith* store trying on some *Tiger Woods* golf shoes.

"Well," I said, "that sounds like the *principle* right there."

A few days later, the decision was made. He was staying. Even after they came back to him with another offer for even more money, he held to his principles.

Very often in leadership we find ourselves emotionally attached to an idea, person, or opportunity that we can allow to overshadow the principles we want to live by.

- Maybe it is an increase in pay or a new title.
- Maybe it's overstepping the budget that your family has set.
- Maybe it's shattering the boundaries with your support staff because you don't think they will do a great job with the responsibilities and autonomy you gave them.
- Maybe it is engaging in a sexual relationship with someone other than your spouse.

172

Whatever it is, it's very easy to compromise our principles. Sticking to principles does not usually result in immediate gain. Feelings and impulses may. But over time, living by principles has the power to bring about sustained growth.

When you find yourself in the midst of a decision, ask yourself "What are my principles?" and move forward.

TRAIN TO BE CLUTCH

- What are 3-5 principles that you want to be known for living out and want to pass on to younger generations?
- Remember Mark Batterson's words, "An opportunity is NOT an opportunity if you have to compromise your integrity"

CHAPTER 56

WILL THIS MATTER IN FIVE YEARS?

THERE ARE A few times in my life that I have been so hungry that all I could think about was FOOD.

One of those times was when I was in Nigeria, Africa.

I had the opportunity to play basketball in Nigeria with an Athletes In Action tour team. We had an extraordinary time with many individual and group experiences.

At night, we often stayed in rooms with 4 people...we talked about many things - girlfriends, basketball, God. But there was one thing that seemed to come up every night...PIZZA.

This probably happened because it seemed that we were always hungry. It was difficult to get food, so we often went to bed feeling hungry.

Throughout the 16-day trip, we had endless debates on which company made the best pizza and which kind of pizza was the best.

These weren't just any conversations about pizza, these pizza conversations were *SERIOUS*. Guys were adamant about their favorite pizza place being the best and would put up a serious defense against anyone who questioned them.

I know it seems trivial NOW, 14 years later, but it was a BIG deal at the time.

What are your "BIG DEALS" right now? Will they *matter* in 5 years?

We create a BIG deal about many things in our lives...

The BIG GAME
The BIG SHOT
The BIG PAY RAISE
The BIG PROMOTION
The BIG DAY

When we think in these terms, we often create *pressure*.

One of the reasons we like pressure is because of the adrenaline rush we get from these events.

The reality is, pressure doesn't exist outside of our mind. We actually create our own pressure.

A beneficial question to ask ourselves, when we are in circumstances that cause our minds to create pressure, is "will this even MATTER in 5 years?"

This helps us to keep the present moment in *PERSPECTIVE* and begin to diffuse the pressure that we are creating in our minds.

As we sing the National Anthem before the championship game what is our focus? If we are focused on the results, winning or losing, and believe that they define us, we begin to create and build up pressure.

It is beneficial to ask ourselves, "Will winning or losing this game *actually* matter in 5 years?"

When you get the ball with 1.8 seconds left in the game, the pressure to make the shot is based on the *significance* YOU have placed on the result. If you make it, you're a hero, if you miss you're a loser.

It is beneficial to ask ourselves, "Will making this last second shot MATTER in 5 years?"

When our boss walks into our office, hands us a case file and tells us that if we do a good job on it, we will finally get a promotion, we create pressure within ourselves because we want the promotion. Completing the case file could come at the cost of our health, our personal life, and our family.

It is beneficial to ask ourselves, "Will spending this time to get this promotion *really* matter in 5 years?"

Before the wedding the bride, groom, parents, and friends are frantically running around trying to get *every* detail of the big day in order.

In the end, the wedding comes and goes and what really matters, is the union of the bride and groom, happens and all the perfect details are a bonus. Whether the roses were on the left side of the stage or on the right side won't MATTER in 5 years. Sometimes it is the things that go **wrong** that *actually* make the best stories down the road.

We turn things in our lives into a big deal, when many times they aren't. It is not to say that there aren't things in our life that are a BIG DEAL, but those moments are few and far between.

It is incredibly valuable to train ourselves to keep a healthy perspective when we find ourselves in circumstances and situations that trigger us to create pressure.

When we can be honest with ourselves with this question, we can have more focus on the present by doing the very best we can, where we are, with what we have in front of us. That is ALL we can do. Do our best regardless of the outcome. This is all that we have control over.

By *consistently training* to have this perspective, we will begin to operate with freedom and will actually be able to perform at a higher level because we are focused on the process and our controllables, which will *decrease* pressure and *increase* confidence.

TRAIN TO BE CLUTCH

- What are some of the things that cause you to feel stress or pressure? Write them out and answer the question: "Will this even matter in 5 years?"

CHAPTER 57

STEWARD SMALL

EVERYONE WANTS TO build the next Apple, *NOBODY* wants to sell matches.

Most people build expenses, not businesses.

Every now and then a person comes along and accidentally gets it the first time, but most of us have to learn the hard way through multiple failed experiments.

Steve Jobs didn't set out to transform entertainment, computers, music, tele-communications, and education. It happened as a byproduct of passion, persistence, and faithfulness to a small idea.

Anson Dorrance didn't set out to win over 20 national championships. It happened as a byproduct of him creating a new NCAA sport, loving his girls, and creating a very competitive environment for them to develop in.

The problem with small ideas is that they aren't sexy.

The guy who won a major golf tournament after getting hit by a bus and doctors telling him he would never walk again said, "Everyone thinks greatness is sexy, it's not. It's dirty, hard work."

Ingvar Kamprad didn't have a sexy idea, he had an idea most people would laugh at today. As a young teenager he started buying matches in bulk and selling them INDIVIDUALLY door-to-door.

I can't even imagine how much grief he took from friends and family. "You are doing WHAT?!!! That is the stupidest idea ever!"

Slowly overtime Ingvar started adding to his inventory, and at the age of 17 he named his business IKEA.

As of November, 2014, almost 80 years later, the brand IKEA is worth $12.5 billion dollars and the 40th most valuable brand in the world.

Everyone wants to build the next IKEA, but nobody wants to sell individual matchsticks door to door.

Everyone wants to build a sports dynasty, but nobody wants to office out of a shed complete with a portable heater like Anson Dorrance did at Carolina for many years AFTER having won over 10 national championships.

Everyone wants to win championships, but nobody wants to sweep their barn that they practice in like John Wooden did for his first few years in Westwood.

Everyone wants to be great, until it's time to do what greatness requires.

Start small.
Be ridiculously faithful.
Focus on what you can control.

*Thanks to JamesClear.com for the story on IKEA

CHAPTER 58

UNCONDITIONAL LOVE

If I ENSLAVED a group of people, treated them horribly, BUT we achieved great things, **Does that make it acceptable??**

NEVER.

Then why do we do this to ourselves?

We must learn how to become our own best friend or best coach.

I'm not talking about never pushing yourself and living by your feelings instead of your principles.

I'm not talking about taking the easy path.

I am talking about learning to love yourself the way God loves you. If you are confused as to what that means, look at how Jesus treated lepers, thieves, and the most downcast in society. His love for us is unconditional, undeserved, and perfectly faithful.

Until we accept His unconditional love for us, it is impossible to love ourselves, and even more impossible to authentically love others and not manipulate them.

Most of what we call love is simply manipulation. Love gives without expecting anything in return and regardless of how it is received. Ask yourself if you would continue to "love" people if they NEVER appreciated, reciprocated, or even acknowledged your love.

Once we accept His love, we can love ourselves, which frees us to freely love.

Achieving "great" things is not an acceptable answer for beating ourselves up and keeping ourselves in a performance-based psychological prison. I would even argue that you are only tapping into a portion of your potential with this strategy and you have no clue what you are capable of if you operated knowing YOU matter, you are loved, you are accepted, and your value comes from who you are, NOT from what you do.

Take the chain off your throat and walk out of the performance based prison by accepting God's free and unconditional love. Talk to yourself the way Jesus is talking to you. If it isn't love, grace, encouraging, and uplifting, then it isn't from Him. Imagine what your days would look like if you talked to yourself the way He talks to you.

TRAIN TO BE CLUTCH

- Study Jesus interactions with people in the New Testament

CHAPTER 59

GOOD NEWS

GROWING UP I was taken to a lot of churches where I was not given good news.

I was given Hell, Fire, Brimstone; a bunch of DO NOT DO lists, sprinkled with a tiny bit of good news around Easter and Christmas.

My hope today is that everywhere I go I bring hope, peace, joy, and the REAL good news that Jesus came to heal and restore. That His love knows no bounds, and that He and His love are passionately, relentlessly, extravagantly, and unconditionally pursuing me, AND you.

He already died and rose again, so anything you did, are doing, or are going to do has already been wiped clean. He asks us to trust in Him and accept and receive this crazy love.

And we do have a choice to not accept the love, but it won't stop Him from continuing to pursue us with His ridiculous love....

God cannot do anything other than love us, because He is love, and He never operates outside of who He is.

If you are unsure of whether you have a choice, and whether or not God could love you, just look at Jesus and Barabbas in the Bible.

Jesus' life was a perfect life full of historically accurate events showing He healed the sick, made the blind see, and raised people from the dead. Jesus' life was freely given so that Barabbas, who was a deplorable member of society, could go free.

Nowhere in the Bible does it say Barabbas ever trusted Jesus with his life; but regardless, Jesus, fully knowing Barabbas would not trust his life to Him, still gave His life so that Barabbas could go free.

God treated Jesus like Barabbas, so that He could treat every human being who will ever live like Jesus.

We must let go of the lies. The Holy Spirit is the great encourager.

The devil is the father of all lies and the great accuser.

Have you ever been around someone who promises you the world but delivers crumbs? That's the devil every time...

We don't know what's good for us, so often times the devil tricks us into believing the cars, the house, and the job are blessings.

Truth is, we don't know what is a blessing and what is a curse. Just ask the people who won the lottery 5 years after they won.

Let go of the lies. Cling to the truth.

TRAIN TO BE CLUTCH

- Listen to the "Jesus is music project" by Judah Smith to learn more about who Jesus REALLY is
- Read *Crash The Chatterbox* by Steven Furtick

CHAPTER 60

WHAT WENT WELL

I'M AMAZED AT how many people in leadership get to the end of their day feeling like very little was accomplished.

What did I do?
What am I doing?
Is any of this making a difference?

I have seen countless people who coach for a living come away from practice, games, and meetings feeling like complete failures. **They spend so much time and energy trying to teach and affect change, yet very rarely see the consistent growth.**

People who are parents often confide in me that at the end of the day they feel like there was nothing they did well that day and quite frequently they just want to crawl up in a ball and cry. The house is a mess, tantrums were thrown throughout the day in public spaces, the dinner is lacking any kind of flavor and you look like a ragamuffin when your spouse comes home.

People in leadership roles in business often say they question their influence and knowledge when it feels like there is little change and movement within their group. Yes the meeting was held but it seems like we are saying the same things over and over, BUT NOTHING CHANGES.

If that's how we feel even 50% of the time, then chances are *we* aren't giving our best to those we lead. It's very likely that we are not seeing the things we do well, and instead we are bombarded with failure after failure. Even if we are not perfectionists, all this lowlight reel does is slip us into a fixed mindset where we start to believe that we have nothing good to offer and our worth comes from what we do.

Remember, our brain is processing over 11 million bits of information, but we are only conscious of about 40 of those bits. We aren't seeing the *WHOLE* picture, not even close.

How great would it be if we had actual feedback on the things we did well?

What if we had a mentor who told us everything we could not see ourselves?

Not many of us have the luxury of having a live-in mentor who does that for us. But we can train ourselves to begin seeing these little victories daily in our lives.

Here's how we do it. ***We don't see what we've done well because we are not consciously surveying our day trying to find those instances.***

If you came to Denver and just walked around you probably wouldn't notice the abundance of Jeep Grand Cherokees that are all around town. But if I asked you to see how many you could count in 10 minutes, you would soon realize that there are at least 3 to 7 at any given intersection. You would SEE them everywhere! They had been there all along, but you needed a fresh perspective to see them.

Much like the arrow in the FedEx logo, the good, the progress, and the stuff we have done has been there all along.

We just need to rewire our brain to consistently see it. The exercise we use to retrain our brain is a "What Went Well" Journal.

If you lack confidence, there is not better exercise than faithfully doing this journal EVERY day, no matter how long it takes. The more that you do it the easier and more natural it will become. In the beginning, it will most likely be very, very hard.

The story you repeatedly tell yourself is the story you will most repeatedly find!

Remember!

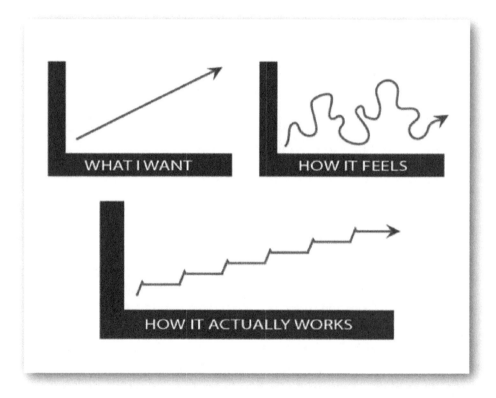

*The how it actually works diagram is the path to mastery from the book, *Mastery*, by George Leonard

Here is the structure we suggest for the journal:

What Went Well Journal
(Rewrite) My value comes from who I am, NOT from what I do.
(Rewrite) Anything that happens to me to-
day is in my best interest
and an opportunity to learn and grow.

Things That I Did Well Today

1. _____
2. _____
3. _____
4. _____
5. _____
6. _____
7. _____
8. _____
9. _____
10. _____
11. _____
12. _____
13. _____
14. _____
15. _____

Areas For Growth

1. _____
2. _____

What I Learned

1. _____
2. _____

Now, let me just say that it is extremely hard for some of us to find 15 things the first time. Most who do later confide in me that they made things up and lied. It takes time to see things more regularly, but as with anything else, consistent practice leads to steady growth.

One of the more important things to realize is that the things you did well do not have to be results. Here are some ideas of things to look for:

- If you are working on letting go of destructive self-talk, write down an instance where you caught yourself using negative self-talk to beat yourself up and decided to stop or say something else.
- If you are working on your body language in the midst of stressful situations, write down your victory in controlling it for at least a minute. Sure it wasn't the whole practice, but it was a step in a more beneficial direction.
- If you are working on your language, write in your journal that you wrote out what you wanted to say on your cue card. You were proactive!
- If you are trying to work on asking good questions and listening, write down that you refused the urge to talk after asking the question.
- If you found yourself comparing yourself to others or arbitrary standards, write out that you became aware of the people or contexts where you are prone to compare. Awareness is half the battle.
- If you chose to read during a busy part of your day, write that down.
- If you set and held your boundary when one of your sweet co-workers came into your office, write that down.
- If you got down on your child's eye level and controlled your emotions as you engaged in talking about unsuitable behavior, write it down.

I know these things are small. But you have to get comfortable with this idea:

ONE IS A WIN!

Even if it was only one time, that is a step in a more beneficial direction. The more that you see the little things that you are doing and growing toward, the more you will see yourself operate in those behaviors again in the future.

Here is the cool part: you are NOT the only one it affects.

One of the guys I get to train plays in the NFL and he does his www journal regularly. In fact, he moved to ninja-status when he started doing it between possessions on the bench. On multiple occasions when the cameras zoom in on him you can see him writing in his journal. I asked him how it was affecting him after a few weeks and he told me it was having a huge affect on how he treated other people.

He plays at the wide receiver position and told me one day, "We came over to the sidelines and I went up to our quarterback and said, 'Hey I know you threw that pick, but you spun the hell out of the ball.'" All his teammate could do was smile, laugh, and move on. In spite of the poor execution, he was able to see the small process-oriented detail that would bring about subsequent completed passes.

People ask all the time about when they should do it. I usually advise doing it after a game, practice, presentation, workshop, or at the end of the day. I say that hesitantly though. A few people who have undergone drastic changes use it *several* times throughout their day. Sometimes they are writing 15 things, other times they are writing 3. One guy who plays college golf does it after practice, between holes, after classes that day and once right before bed.

Regardless of *when* you do it, the important thing is that you simply do it. If you play golf, or do some other activity, business included, where you can keep track of your what went wells as you go, then we suggest doing it as you go! But there is nothing that says you cannot do it during your water break during a team practice!

At UCLA women's basketball What Went Well journals are a mandatory part of the end of every practice. Remember, we make time for what we value.

If we are changing how we see ourselves, and if the axiom is true that we judge others by the same measure we judge ourselves, then it brings a lot of hope and excitement as we look toward the future and the growth of our family, team, and organization. As you start to become more comfortable catching yourself doing it well, you will become more comfortable catching other people doing it well!

I'll finish with this: the people who do the journal consistently for at least 3 to 6 weeks **do not** remain the same.

TRAIN TO BE CLUTCH

- When are you going to make time to do your Journal today?
- When can you encourage your team or group to do it corporately?
- Inside your brain, false memories quickly become just as true, in your estimation, as real ones.[7]

---

7 Brain Works, The mind-bending science of how you see, what you think, and who you are. Michael S. Sweeney. National Geographic

CHAPTER 61

A SIMPLE TEXT SPARKED A FIRE

I WAS TALKING to Joshua one day about a concept that got me really excited for one of the books we are working on. I sent him a message and asked him about the concept and he replied that he wanted to unpack it further and that we probably shouldn't talk about it on Twitter until we talked together.

I agreed.

About 2 minutes later I got a text from him that said, **"I love when you get fired up and create stuff!"**

What's really interesting is that for a long time what he and I both said to each other was:

Have you written that article yet?
Have you written the article yet?
Have you written THAT article yet?!!

And what happens a lot of times is that I get so *frustrated* and feel so *guilty* about writing that the process becomes a "Have To" and sometimes the writing never gets done.

This day was different.

It was one of the toughest days I'd had in a while in terms of energy, but after Joshua sent me that text I got excited about creating more. That night, between 8:30 and 9:45, while watching Thursday Night Football, I was able to write 3 articles that ended up being pretty helpful to others.

Instead of **telling me** to write an article or making me feel guilty about it he actually **praised me** and said he loves to watch me create!

He didn't sap my energy. He gave me energy!!!!

What could happen if you stopped telling your team, "Hey we need more effort! We need more energy! The focus isn't good enough!"

What could happen if you stopped asking your employees, "Have you filled out those reports yet?"

What could happen if you stopped asking your wife, "Did you fill up the car with gas?"

What could happen if you stopped asking your husband, "Have you started on that list yet?"

What if you started to tell them:

"Man you brought energy today! I love to watch you compete! I love to watch you work hard! I'm so happy you chose our team."

"Babe, I love when you find a way to get stuff done even though you are juggling everything on your plate!"

"Babe, I love when you do the yard work and fix stuff around the house, it really turns me on."

Those simple and sincere compliments most often are **devoid of judgment.**
They are not a shot at who someone is.
They are not threatening.

When people don't feel judged, they usually feel energized to continue to fan into flame the things that they do really well.

It's been shown that whatever you focus on in relationships tends to grow overtime.

Will you focus and encourage what they do well, or dwell on their weaknesses?

There is a time for correction and discipline, but if we aren't careful our voice can become a nagging one that actually reinforces the behaviors we are asking to change.

A specific and sincere compliment can change the entire trajectory of someone's life.

Transformational leadership is about making those we lead *feel* like we believe in them more than they believe in themselves. Sometimes in life, we need to talk less and love more.

Whose spark will you fan into a flame today?

TRAIN TO BE CLUTCH

- Write out 2 people you know you will interact with today. Write down something they bring to the table or do well. Write out a simple sentence (NOT A PARAGRAPH) you can share with them that focuses on what they do well.

- Remind yourself of what you do well by writing a WWW Journal at least once a day.
- People's memories are not only formed from all that they have done, but they are also the sum of what they have been told and hence believe.

CHAPTER 62

THE DARK SIDE OF LEADERSHIP

IT IS RARELY talked about until it explodes.

Sometimes I think it is even celebrated.

The dark side of leadership are the insecurities and traumas a person experiences, especially at a young age, that end up fueling their relentless drive and passion to *"prove they are good enough"* for the rest of their life.

Gary McIntosh and Samuel Rima share a puzzling thought:

"A significant number of leaders of the past and present came from rigid homes with unrealistic standards and a perfectionistic parent who withheld approval and signs of love until those perfect standards were attained. This type of environment threatens the need that children have to feel approved and accepted by the most important people in their life— their parents. This withholding of love or lack of demonstrable approval by a parent for whatever reason creates a deep hole within the personality of the child and may launch him or her on a life quest to gain the approval of that parent." -Gary L. McIntosh & Samuel D. Rima Sr. "Overcoming the Dark Side of Leadership."

The sad part is that without acknowledging and working through those issues no amount of money, success, or fame ever truly heals those wounds. Similar to when a bone is broken, or a muscle is pulled, the body compensates for the injury. We do the same thing psychologically, but often times the compensation never stops making it bigger and bigger. Many times whatever continues to grow out of control is fueled by anger, jealousy, bitterness, unforgiveness, hatred, and ultimately fear.

Sometimes it is empathy, other times it is drive, ambition, courage, reckless abandon, perfectionism, or the compensation that can take on many other forms that are most often celebrated as your greatest strength.

What you have to realize is that the area of your greatest strength can just as easily be the area of your greatest weakness. Without balance, some other area often explodes. We see this all the time with people in leadership who have extramarital affairs, or drug habits, or many other falls from grace.

"People who ignore or refuse to acknowledge their dark side frequently encounter major failures in their leadership responsibilities." -Gary L. McIntosh & Samuel D. Rima Sr. "Overcoming the Dark Side of Leadership"

Recycling our pain and using it to for beneficial causes is a wonderful thing, but we must always be aware of our dark side. Not only do we need to have high levels of self-awareness, but we also need to setup safety measures to guard against potential challenges.

Personally, I know that my greatest strengths are also my greatest weaknesses, and I have to be aware of it every day in everything that I do. I know that my desire to push forward and be the best in the world at what we do can cause me to overlook people who don't operate at a certain level. I know that barreling forward can cause me to miss opportunities to slow down and simply be there for people who are clearly and deeply hurt. But it is that same desire to be the best in the world that helps me push aside naysayers and do things that other people say we cannot do.

Again, our greatest strengths can be our greatest weaknesses, and we need to be aware of it in everything we do.

Here are a few suggestions for overcoming your dark side.

1.) Work with a psychotherapist or counselor to help you unveil some of the deeper issues that are driving your actions.
2.) Spend time every day reading material that is going to fuel your heart in beneficial ways.
3.) Try to journal or write letters when you are frustrated. Abraham Lincoln would write a letter to the person he was angry with, but then he would never actually mail the letter. Warren Buffett says, sleep on it, you don't lose the right to tell someone off tomorrow.
4.) Schedule times of silence, rejuvenation, and recovery every month. I start my day with gratefulness prayer and meditation for this reason. I also try and pick two times of the year to spend extended time away for recovery after basketball and my speaking circuits.
5.) Exercise. Too many people in leadership are jeopardizing their ability to lead through their health. Without your health, money, freedom, and other joys are very meaningless.
6.) Forming an inner circle of trusted advisors who will challenge you. We wrote about this topic in our first book, _Burn Your Goals_, you can read the chapter here http://www.traintobeclutch.com/who-is-in-your-circle-change-your-circle-change-your-life/

Your dark side can be a very valuable tool and often will push you and create a fire inside of you to conquer any obstacle that stands in your way. The challenge is to channel it and make sure it doesn't implode because it was never managed. The dark side can be your greatest ally, but it is also your greatest enemy.

Be aware of it.
Take steps to protect against it.
Channel it.
Work through it.

And most importantly have people around you that are willing and able to help you get out of your own way so that you can truly become a person committed to transformational leadership in both word and deed. Don't be the person whose mission is to be a transformational leader but your family is falling apart because they never get your best love, time, and energy.

TRAIN TO BE CLUTCH

- Read, *Overcoming the Dark Side of Leadership* by Gary L. McIntosh & Samuel D. Rima Sr.

CHAPTER 63

ADJUST YOUR WARRIOR DIAL

WOULDN'T IT BE great to have a tool that helps you manage your emotions? I had the pleasure to sit down and listen to a guy who served as a Navy SEAL who shared some wisdom with me on how he does just that.

There were a lot of things he mentioned, but there was one tool he shared that blew my mind! I've been using it almost daily since he spoke and it has radically altered my interactions with others.

He told me that one of the things he constantly practiced in his training missions was the ability to regulate his emotions. And a tool he used for it was what he called *the warrior dial.*

In battle all sorts of things could happen. You could be coming from just having seen someone in your team having had one of their limbs blown off, and or killed, and as you are entering the next building, the room could be filled with women and children. If your emotions are running at a 10 from what you just experienced, you could think about turning a dial down somewhere around a 5 so as to think and execute with clarity.

- How helpful would it be for you to adjust your dial after making an errant pass to calm yourself down?
- How helpful would it be for you to adjust your dial to let go of a frustrating administration meeting before stepping onto the court with your team?

- How helpful would it be for you to adjust your dial after a frustrating day as you step into your home to be with your family?
- How helpful would it be for you as a parent to adjust your dial before bedtime when your child is trying to stall and play with toys?
- How helpful would it be to adjust your dial before walking into that big merger meeting?
- How helpful would it be to adjust your dial before walking into that big interview?

As I write this article, my son is literally driving his toy truck up the back of my Mac Book Pro. I can be short with him, or take a second to assess my warrior dial and dial it back to a place where I can operate out of love and joy.

What I do is ask myself
"What's my number right now?"
"Where is the most *beneficial* place for me to be?"

I take a few controlled breaths. Adjust my posture. Assume a non-judgmental facial expression. And then move forward giving my best.

Sure it's not necessarily how I *feel*, but it is the most beneficial way for me to intentionally operate for my family, teams, and with my team at Train To Be CLUTCH.

CHAPTER 64

ABSORB THE ANXIETY

I WILL NEVER forget this day in Ireland. It was at the height of the economic crisis in Europe and it was right in the middle of our semester at the Irish Bible Institute.

Ireland had gone from one of the fastest growing economies in the world, to one of the worst economies in Europe in about two years. There were companies going bankrupt left, right and center. Banks were even being nationalized. Everywhere you looked in the papers and on television was doom and gloom.

I remember we were eating lunch in the café at the college when our founder and head master walked in and asked for our attention. We were a small college that was largely run off of donations and our future looked very bleak.

Jacob called our attention while holding his cup of tea and gave one of the most profound talks I have ever heard.

He told us that though things looked bleak in the economy, he was sure in who God was. He had seen God provide in his life and reminded us to remember God's hand in our lives. He told us not to worry about the future of IBI, but to remain faithful to our studies and seeking God's will in our lives. He said it was his job to speak with people about funding and it was God's role of being the provider.

It was not so much of what he said, but it was really about how he made me feel. It was as if in that moment someone had woken me up from the bad dream and I realized things weren't so scary.

He didn't promise grandiose things that he couldn't deliver on. He didn't dwell on how we should not worry. But with conviction in who God is, he absorbed every ounce of anxiety that was in my soul.

His talk couldn't have been more than a minute. But the way he carried himself made me feel like it was a foregone conclusion that the funding would arrive. And it did. They received more money in donations than they had ever received before.

I was talking with one my friends who coaches at a high level that I love being around and he told me that the most impactful thing I have taught him was about absorbing the anxiety. Body Language, heart posture, language, and beliefs all play into this ability. But it is the one thing that has the ability to develop confidence and conviction in those we get to lead.

It causes others outside of our team to wonder what we know that they don't. It's the one thing that genuinely connects me to people I would run through walls for.

It's not promising wins and success. It's not casting grandiose visions about what could be. It's about operating with a belief that you are commissioned and called to lead where you are. It's about leading because you are compelled by love for those you get to serve. And it is operating with conviction that trusting in God and operating by principles will carry your group through hell and high water.

Know that you are commissioned.
Be compelled by love.
Operate with conviction.
Absorb the anxiety.

CHAPTER 65

NO HYPE NEEDED

I ALWAYS THOUGHT I needed to get pumped up for the BIG game, so I would watch, *Braveheart*, and listen to rap music, then I would usually get red carded and ejected from the game before the conclusion.

I didn't need to be listening to upbeat music, watching an inspirational movie, or hear an Al Pacino Any Given Sunday pre-game speech. I actually needed the exact opposite before most big games.

I needed to listen to classical music, take a lot of deep breathes, and lower my heart rate.

If you want to become a transformational leader then you need to understand this clearly. BIG games, BIG client meetings, or any other high intensity moments don't need you to make them any bigger. What your team needs from you is for you to take the pressure off and for them to remember it's not a big deal in the grand scheme of life.

Too many times we burn off so much energy in the emotions of the BIG event that we are exhausted by the time it actually gets here, and we are drained of our much needed resources to be at our best.

It's the little events where those in leadership need to manufacture energy and give the really emotionally charged speeches, not the other way around. How many times have you seen a clearly better team beaten by a lesser opponent....they needed that manufactured energy.

Most of the time what your team needs from you as the leader is for you to calm them down, not to fire them up.

"What I discovered playing for the Knicks is that when I got too excited mentally, it had a negative effect on my ability to stay focused under pressure. So I did the opposite. Instead of charging players up, I developed a number of strategies to help them quiet their minds and build awareness so they could go into battle poised and in control." — Phil Jackson, *Eleven Rings: The Soul of Success*

TRAIN TO BE CLUTCH

- What are some examples of a team you have been a part of where a person or a whole team burned out quickly because they were over hyped?
- What are some things you can do to help those you lead calm down besides deep breathing exercises and classical music?

CHAPTER 66

WHAT TO DO WHEN YOU ARE HAVING ONE OF THOSE DAYS

"Practice was horrible. I mean really, really *bad*," she said, and all the other girls on the team agreed.

"Let me ask you this," I said. "What is your measure for whether or not practice was *good*?"

One girl said, "That it's functional and you feel sharp. Mainly you get something out of it."

"I'd challenge you on that one," I said. "What if your measure for a good practice was that your failures outweighed your successes?"

Blank faces all around and most likely thinking, "Are you kidding me?!! Who is *this* freaking guy!?!"

Funny enough, this conversation was right before we listened to a guy who retired from the Navy SEALs talk about how hard his training was for 2.5 years. He told us that he had a 50-meter swim he had to complete without surfacing. The only way to fail the test was to surface before touching the wall.

He paused, smiled, and said, "I chose not to surface."

That's right, he passed out in the water!

His training was set toward failure. And he said that there was nothing in live battle that was as hard as his training had ever been!

What if we came to practice with the focus of doubling our rate of failure? I'm not talking about lazy or thoughtless mistakes. I'm talking about going so hard that you are operating on the edges of your ability. I'm talking about taking on challenges that are not easy. Choosing 1v1 drills against the best person on the team. Choosing to run beside the fastest person on the team.

Yes, you may fail. But if we are only doing things that are somewhat comfortable, we will never scratch our true potential.

You are going to feel like you are so exhausted you are going to puke. Do you want to feel weak and exhausted in training, or when you are playing on TV under the bright lights?!

You are going to feel exposed and unprepared for certain questions and arguments. Do you want to feel that way in training or when you are pitching a massive potential client?

If you coach, how do you measure whether or not practice was good?

I had a person who coaches at the Division 1 level tell me that the whole team came to practice the other day lacking in energy and focus. They have instituted many of our tools to help their team adjust, but "Jamie, what do you do in THAT situation?"

"Let me ask you this," I said, "how many games in past seasons has this same lack in focus occurred?"

"More than a few games."

So, if it's very likely that the majority of our team will have a night like this, then we need to help _**equip**_ them to adjust.

First, we need to have a shift in perspective.

If you notice that the majority of the team is struggling in this way, let's decide as a staff that a successful practice will now be that we help them adjust their focus. Never mind, points, efficiency of inbound plays, or tactics. Today's focus is helping them adjust their mental state.

Second, we need to encourage failure.

One of the things we have the power to do is take the edge and threat off of the game. The people you are leading are most likely frustrated that they cannot adjust and that things are seemingly getting worse.

As the person coaching I would encourage you to smile and say, "Look, it's tough right? Can we all agree that we are struggling? This is part of the game. I am not looking for perfect practice. Let's think of how we can change things because this is going to help us adjust in games later in the season."

Encourage them that no one, myself included, comes with 100% focus and energy every second of every day. We are not looking for perfection. We are looking for the ability to exercise self-control and get better today.

Third, we need to give them a specific focal point for a short period of time.

Instead of having the team ra-ra and demand that everyone picks it up, give them 2, and no more than 2, things to focus on for the next minute. (I would encourage that loud communication be one of the focal points because this is where most of these breakdowns happen. Most of the time we get quiet or start screaming things that are not helpful when we are frustrated.)

After **1 minute**, come back and ask them what changed. Give them the focal points again and let them go out longer this time.

I did this while coaching in Ireland. My team had not lost a game that season and we were about to play the worst team in the league. During warm up our team was very sluggish and the guys were getting frustrated because the level was not high. So in the middle of play, I picked up the ball. I just looked at everyone and calmly said, "Guys, can we all agree that this has all the signs of us being about ready to get rolled over?"

The guys mostly nodded. I said to focus on loud communication and man-to-man defense for the next minute. Everyone was buzzing around for that minute and the entire atmosphere changed. We went out and played extremely well straight from the tip-off.

So let me challenge you again:

What is your measure for a practice being good?

CHAPTER 67

YOU DON'T KNOW WHAT YOU HAVE UNTIL IT'S GONE

AN ELDERLY MAN was called up to the podium at church one day to share his thoughts before we took the Lord's Supper. He hobbled up there, adjusted the microphone, took a deep breath to speak, and paused in silence. It was one of those moments where you knew emotions were going to flow.

"I've been around for a few years on this earth, and in that time I've learned a thing or two. But it hasn't been until my knees started to give, my kids all moved away, and my wife passed that I realized the painful truth of the cliché: *you never know what you have until it's gone....*

Every day I sit and think about my son when he was 2 and all the energy he had as we played baseball and soccer together. He would be over the moon when he saw a trash truck come and collect the garbage. He'd get those big eyes, throw his arms out wide and yell "Big truck!"

He chuckled in remembrance.

"I think about the days when I was playing with my team. We'd show up to practice on hot days and just complain about what the coach would have us do. When others made a mistake we'd poke fun and laugh. But when it was time to play, the guys fought tooth and nail to help each other out."

He shook his head in disbelief.

"I also think about my wife."

His voice trembled as his eyes welled up.

"I miss her so much! She used to make me breakfast every morning even when she didn't feel like it. She loved nothing more than to cuddle with me on the couch and watch a movie. She would always give me a pat on the *'tush'* when I walked by her or gave her a kiss. She'd ask me to read and I'd get to watch her fall asleep every night."

He sniffles, breathes, and is finally able to look us in the eyes.

"The hard part is....I took most of those things for granted. Most of my thoughts were about the things I didn't have, or the experiences we couldn't have, or the problems or obstacles that were holding us back. I can tell you this.....I'd give *anything* to watch the trash be collected with my son. I'd give all of my money to be able to run around and play sports again for one day. And I would work all day every day for just one moment with my wife to tell her how much I love her.

It's simple y'all, we don't realize what we have until it's gone. And today we get to celebrate the greatest gift of all. God created us, Jesus cleansed us, and the Holy Spirit lives inside of us. I don't care what else is happening to, in, or around us. But that's awesome. Let's give thanks!"

What would today look like if you spent 2 minutes writing out what you are grateful for in the morning?

My dad was diagnosed with terminal cancer when he was 49 years old. I watched as he gained a whole new perspective on life. He loved people deeper, he said I love you more, and people became one of his top priorities.

Imagine if one of the people you lead were to kill themselves. Would you be able to look back and be proud of the way you coached them? That exact scenario happened to one of the people we work with.

Imagine if you lost one of your kids. Would you regret all the days you stayed at the office late and the important events you didn't make a priority? *Would you regret giving them the life you never had rather than the parent they desperately craved?*

Imagine if your daughter has to walk down the aisle without you. Would you regret not making your health a priority?

After watching what happened to my dad, I made a commitment at 21 years old. Don't wait until you have cancer to appreciate EVERYTHING God has given you. Enjoy it all: the highs, the lows, the tough stuff, the painful stuff, and the fun stuff. Live in a perpetual state of gratitude. *I want to be able to get diagnosed with terminal cancer and it not change a thing about the way I live.*

CHAPTER 68

THE DANGER OF COMFORTABLE

SOMETIMES WE GET to this place where we are really comfortable, and we want to get to the next level, but **what we *really* want is to not mess it all up.**

We slowly slip into this state where we play not to lose, instead of playing to win.

We all know what happens when a team uses this strategy.

We find ourselves in a place where we think we are grateful to be there, but it's not truly gratefulness. No, it is fear masquerading as gratefulness.

If we are honest we think we are lucky to have made it to where we are, and if luck had something to do with it, then we don't want to mess it all up, because we could lose it all, and maybe luck won't be on our side the next time around.

Without knowing it we start listening to the self-defeating gremlins in our head that tell us we are just a *fraud*, we don't really belong, and sooner than later *everyone* is going to find out.

We rob the world and those around us of precious wisdom and value because we don't think we have something of value to offer. We think we lack the resources required to make something that others will benefit from, or we fall into dangerous land of "someday" I will create it, write it, or give it, but I don't have enough value today.

So....

We postpone writing the book the world needs to read.

We don't mentor that person who was just like us.

We don't create that thing that we wish we had.

We don't experiment with a potential solution.

Sadly, it doesn't matter if we are working with a 14 year-old kid, or a "super successful" adult in sports or business; almost everyone suffers from this "not good enough" disease.

We think when we are younger that if we just ACHIEVE enough or GET enough _____, the voices in our head and the self-defeating thoughts will go away.

They don't.

Not if you don't learn how to combat them and train yourself to operate differently.

We slowly start to operate out of fear rather than love. When we started out, we naively wanted to change the world and our love of people and making a difference is what drove us. In the beginning we had nothing to lose so we were willing to take risks and go against the status quo. It was this willingness to go for it that got us to where we are, not luck. **It was our faithfulness, not fortune.**

Now we are established.
We make good money.
We are comfortable.

We finally got a starting spot on the team.
We have a family to think about.
We have the corner office.

We don't want to mess it up.

You know you aren't fulfilling your potential, but fulfilling your potential requires taking risks that seem so much bigger now.

We are afraid that if we rock too hard we might be the ones to fall out of the boat, struggling to survive like all the people we see out of the boat floating around with nothing but a barely inflated life vest.

It's amazing how quickly pride and fear can masquerade as practicality or wisdom.

If I truly adopt a growth mindset that means I believe EVERYTHING that happens to me is in my best interest and an opportunity to learn and grow. When I got knocked out in San Diego I was scared to death about losing everything I had built, but it was that story and my willingness to be authentically vulnerable with people about it that opened so many more doors.

Growth is only on the other side of comfortability. *I cannot grow unless I am seeking out the toughest challenges at the edges of my ability.*

If I'm comfortable I'm most likely doing something that is less than beneficial.
If YOU are comfortable, you are most likely doing something that is less than beneficial.

CHAPTER 69

THE DANGER OF SOMEDAY

WHEN I STARTED playing soccer, all I could dream about was scoring a goal. Playing in my first season where we lost at least 7-0 every game, my desire to celebrate a goal was unfathomable! I thought that day was going to be the best day of my life!

Well, I scored from midfield against the sharks! It was sweet, but short-lived.

From there, all I wanted was to win a tournament. I'd seen everyone we played with patches of tournaments they had won sewn on their shorts, and I would look down at my shorts, patch-less, and feel dejected. But then I joined a new team with a forward who ran a 4.2 40 meter and the first tournament saw us wearing the medals and smiling.

From there all I wanted was to win a state championship. I wanted it so bad that I would dream of it ever single night as I did sit ups in my bed while heading a ball hanging from my brother's top bunk. No joke. It's all I thought about, and now there are easily 5 state championship medals in a box somewhere in my parents' house.

After that, winning a regional final was next on the bill. That was achieved and the only thing I really remember about it was the 2 sizes-too-big-jacket they gave us as a prize.

This continued on for a good few years until it finally came to a head. My team in Ireland was fast becoming the most dominant team in the country leading us all the way to FAI Junior Final (national champion-ship) at Tolka Park. The day was magical. Fans singing, the ball zipping across one of the nicest fields in the country, and a top-class opponent.

I was dominant that day. Hardly anything came through the mid-field where I played. I won countless tackles and headers. And I rang quite possibly the hardest shot of my life off the crossbar from 35 yards out. In unison, the crowd all shouted "Ooooohhhhh."

I actually walked away not only having won a national title, but I was named the Man of the Match. It was pretty cool to have a crowd of Irish fellas all chanting "U-S-A!"

I remember a fan and very strong supporter of the club coming up to me afterwards. He was beaming from ear to ear as he pulled me in close. He looked at me and said, "Jamie, remember this. This will be the best day of your life."

With all due respect, it wasn't. None of those days were. *Those achieve-ments and what they represented were fun, but they didn't bring fulfillment. If I'm honest, all those achievements did is leave me wanting more. Like drinking a soda, they actually left me more dehydrated than I was before them.*

The night I scored my first goal was also the night I did my spelling homework and filled our dishwasher with dirty dishes.

After we won our state tournament I was the one with the Shout stain-stick trying to get the grass stains out of my uniform.

After we were crowned as one of the top 4 teams in the country, I am quite certain I paid the same $9.95 as everyone else for the buffet at Ruby Tuesdays.

After the FAI final I sat with Amy on the windowsill of Little Caesar's on the Ballymun Road scarfing the pizza *we* paid for. Maybe we didn't see them, but the paparazzi wasn't around. There were no autographs. No perks. And the next morning I walked to the train and worked all day making sushi and selling coffee.

I have found that many of us have a "Someday" statement or two in our lives.

- "Someday, when we become a top 10 program then I will spend less time in the office and more time at home."
- "Someday, when I finally get on top of all my emails I will start to spend more time reading books."
- "Someday, when I get $____ in the bank then I will feel safe and secure."
- "Someday, when my son is older and can do cool stuff, then I will make more time to be around him."
- "Someday, when I make more money then I will give some away to people in need."
- "Someday, when we win a championship then I will be remembered and revered as a great coach."

If we are not careful we can spend so much time and effort focused on the destination that we miss out on the journey.

It's not the trophy that makes me smile and fills me with joy each day. I literally, use it as a doorstop! It's not the comments people make when they introduce me to others as a "baller" or "one of the best they ever played with" that bring value to my life.

It's the relationships I made, cultivated, and sustained over the years that bring so much joy to my life.

As I look forward it is easy to believe that buying our first home, working with one of the biggest athletic departments in the country, writing another book, or getting my custom KD's made will bring fulfillment and lasting joy. But wisdom raises her voice.

TRAIN TO BE CLUTCH

- List out 3 of your own "Someday" statements.
- What has this "someday" focus and cost you in your present day?
- Who do you *get to* be around today that you can thank, love on, or be specific and sincere with?

CHAPTER 70

PERSPECTIVE

LUKE IS 15 years old and he is one of the happiest people around. Yet he can't walk, talk, or feed himself. Luke is my brother. Luke helps me regain perspective on what TRULY matters in life.

Luke has taught me some extremely valuable lessons in life:

Lesson 1- Use what you have

So many times I get caught up and focus on all the things I don't have in life, and in doing so I make myself miserable. The sad part is it doesn't matter how much or how little your or I have, because there will always be someone who seems to have more than us.

As the philosopher Chris Brown said, "The grass is greener where you water it."

Luke lives by this philosophy and he definitely makes the most of what he has and is able to do. He loves to try and dunk a small ball in his little tikes goal. He loves for you to get down on his level and wrestle with him. He loves to play catch, and by catch I mean, get hit with the ball, and then throw it nowhere near you! He can't talk, but he can growl and point. And while he sometimes get's frustrated with us for not understanding him, usually he just keeps growling until you get the point. Which brings me to the second lesson.

Lesson 2- Persist no matter what obstacles you face

Luke is the most persistent person I know. He will literally growl, point, and even yell until he gets your attention to do what he wants. If you tell him no, or that you're busy, he just keeps on growling and pointing, until eventually you relent. I often wonder how different my life would be if I showed the same level of persistence in pursuing the things I am passionate about.

Lesson 3- Laugh when you mess up

Luke loves when people fall over, get tackled, or when someone drops something, he belly laughs so hard, you can't help but laugh along with him. He laughs at mistakes. When he misses a dunk, he doesn't care. He just wants to do it again. He loves the act of trying and relishes every moment regardless of the outcome.

Sometimes I have a tendency to take things way too seriously, when I need to take a play from Luke's playbook and just laugh at the mistake and try again.

An interesting side note: We tend to get frustrated when people forget something we have taught them, or if we or they make a mistake on things already learned. But do we do this with little kids learning to walk? NO! We would never tell them how stupid they are for falling down and that we already taught them how to walk last week. We encourage them, and we usually do it with a smile. I wonder what would happen if we used that same approach with ourselves and those we lead?

Lesson 4- Love unconditionally and SMILE more

One of my favorite things when I get home from a trip is coming home to Luke! He is like a dog in that he loves unconditionally, and when you get home he acts like it is the biggest deal in the world! He often squeals like a little pig, throws his arms out wide, and has the biggest smile on his face, and he desperately wants to give you a hug. Almost everyone who has ever met Luke falls in love with him. His capacity for love comes deep within his heart, and it flows out on everyone he's around.

As I write this, I have tears welling up in my eyes. Here is a kid who can't do so many things we take for granted every day, yet he is able to have an immeasurable impact on the world from a wheelchair. I think he enjoys the few things he is able to do in life more than we enjoy everything we get to do.

Luke helps me have a much healthier perspective on life.

Who helps you have perspective on what really matters in life?

CHAPTER 71

TRAINING TO *GET* BETTER VS. TRAINING TO *FEEL* BETTER

I HONESTLY COULDN'T believe it.

I was about to tell a woman who had been on the LPGA tour for 16 years that she wasn't practicing to get better; she was practicing to feel better. And so were Michelle Wie and all the other ladies I had just watched practice on the putting green for the last 2 hours.

You see, deliberate practice is hard. It is frustrating, and it forces you to operate at the edges of your ability. It is what very few people consistently engage in.

Most people practice to feel better. They will spend hours and hours in the gym, at the office, on the driving range, all in an effort to "build their confidence." Then those same people are often inconsolable when they crumble under pressure, and don't understand how the world could be so cruel, because after all, they "deserved to win" after all the hard work and sacrifice they made.

The problem is they aren't putting themselves in similar or more challenging environments than what they will compete in. They are putting themselves in cushy situations where they create a false sense of confidence.

Let me give you some examples of the difference.

Practicing to feel better:

Golf- Hitting putt after putt from the same spot. Hitting shot after shot with the same club in your hand on the driving range.

Think about this......If player B (the person who hit the mulligan during the round of golf) has at least a million more bits of information than player A, then hitting 50 seven irons on the range, or 50 three footers from the same spot, gives you a completely false sense of security and inflated sense of ability going into competitive rounds. This then leads to increased frustration because your on-course performance never lives up to how the player with a million times more information hits the ball on the range and on the putting green.

Basketball- Shooting hundreds of shots in the gym by yourself.

Business- Practicing your sales pitch hundreds of times to your colleagues.

Training to GET better:

Golf- Never hitting a putt from the same place. Never hitting the same shot twice on the driving range, constantly changing clubs and never allowing yourself to get comfortable. Doing something to get your heart rate up in between every few shots. Playing the three-hole stretch over and over again at your local course that forces you to work on the shots that you have struggled with in competition. For example, hitting a really tight fairway with out of bounds to the right, and water to the left. Having to hit over water to a green with a 150-yard carry.

Basketball- Shooting game shots, from game spots at game speed. Not just getting the ball from the shooting machine, but facing the opposite direction and having to listen and spin around before catching and shooting. Setting up cones and chairs and coming off a fake screen before taking shots. Having someone distract you with pots and pans and all sorts of other distractions as you shoot free throws. Never shooting more than 3 free throws at a time without stepping away from the line.

Business- going out to the mall and practicing your pitch to random strangers that are walking around.

Before I did my first ever wedding, for one of my best friends, I was in the bathroom practicing with all the groomsmen and told them they could do anything they wanted to distract me while I practiced. I was comfortable speaking in public, but I knew I would be out of my normal comfort zone and I needed to train in that environment to be more comfortable when it counted.

The ancient Greek philosophers used to practice giving speeches with rocks in their mouths, in order to perfect their craft. As the modern day philosopher from the movie, *Dodgeball*, put it, "If you can dodge a wrench, you can dodge a ball."

Basically, you never want to get comfortable in training. As soon as you get comfortable you want to increase the challenge so that you are operating at the edges of your ability. You are going to feel uncomfortable at some point, the problem is, too many people feel uncomfortable during the important moments because they have failed to consistently make themselves uncomfortable during training.

TRAIN TO BE CLUTCH

- What are ways in your business, relationships, or sport that you train to "feel" better instead of actually get better?
- What can you do to change that?

CHAPTER 72

HOW ARE *WE* MODELING THE PROBLEM?

A PERSON WHO coaches that I get to work with walked over to me and said, "What should I do if I'm not supposed to run them?! Every single one of them showed up with their shirts untucked..... I would make them run in the past, but *you say* we shouldn't use fitness as a punishment."

I looked at him and tried be as humble as possible as I said, "please look at you and your staff."

Every one of their shirts were un-tucked.

They are always learning, but we aren't always aware of what we are teaching.

I hear people in coaching and education complaining about entitlement, awful mindset, and many other issues, but I've rarely heard them say...."**Maybe we are part of the problem.**"

John Wooden said, "Young people need models, not critics." I completely agree, and would take it one step further. *PEOPLE* need models, not critics. Anyone can be a critic, it is ridiculously hard to be a model.

TRAIN TO BE CLUTCH

- What are your biggest challenges in the team you lead?
- In what ways could you or your support staff be modeling those problems?

CHAPTER 73

MARGIN MADNESS

STEPHANIE AND I were walking into the post office to mail some books and the man sitting on the ground outside asked if he could draw us a picture when we came back out.

10 minutes later we walked out and I said, "Alright, draw us a picture."

I assumed 2 or 3 minutes later we would have a little drawing, I would give him a few bucks, and we would be on our way.

45 minutes later this guy was still working on our black and white charcoal portrait. We both learned a little bit about each other's stories, and he gave some really good evidence for why he preferred living on the street instead of shelters.

Having served at the *Dream Center,* having sat on the board for *Broken Hearts,* and having slept on *Skidrow* myself, Zachary and I had more in common than either one of us might have thought at the outset.

A few days before that experience I had listened to Carl Lentz give a talk about "margin madness." He talked about how most of us have no margin in our life, so we never have anything extra to give.

This was extremely challenging for me, because for most of my life I had lived in that exact manner, ESPECIALLY in the area of finances.

I lived paycheck to paycheck, never creating any financial margin. When I made more money, I spent it. When I had extra money, I felt like it was an opportunity to splurge. Inevitably, I ended up in a similar financial situation every month regardless of how much money I had made.

"If the devil cannot kill you by getting you to do bad things, he will distract and destroy you by getting you busy doing good things." -Carl Lentz

As I wrote about in the beginning of this book, I think busyness is a new form of laziness. If you tell me you don't have time for your priorities, then I would say it's time to create better margin in your life.

Stephen Covey stresses the importance of "scheduling our priorities instead of prioritizing our schedule." I would say almost nothing is more important. It's what we call putting first things first.

If we aren't careful we can get so caught up doing the most *pressing* thing that we forget or suppress the most *important* things.

This is how our health goes to waste.

This is how our families feel we don't care about them.

This is how our team feels like they are just production units.

Thankfully, I had created enough margin in my life that I had time, money, and books to give Zachary the day I met him outside the post office, because so many times in my life I've had no margin and had nothing left to give emotionally, physically, spiritually, financially, nor any extra time in which to give them.

It's time we stop operating with margin madness and start taking intentional steps every day toward creating margin so when opportunity tugs on our heart we actually have something to freely give.

Creating healthy margins in your life might just end up saving your family, your business, your marriage, or your life.

TRAIN TO BE CLUTCH

- What area do you need to create more margin in today?
- What have you sacrificed by not having any margin in this area of your life?
- What are 3 things you can do today to start creating margin in this area?
- What is one thing you plan to say NO to today?

CHAPTER 74

TRAINING FOR YOUR MOMENT VS. WAITING FOR YOUR MOMENT

How WOULD YOU use your 86,400 seconds today, if you knew you were going to get the opportunity of your dreams??

While many people are waiting for their opportunity, a few people are preparing for theirs!

Have you ever heard of a Boom Boat?

My uncle grew up on Vancouver Island, BC and had gotten a job at the local Pulp Mill.

Being a young guy, he was given the job of Laborer.

My uncle loves to learn, especially when it comes to figuring out how things operate.

One day he noticed these tiny, one-man boats out in the water that were used to gather logs together. He asked the guy standing next to him, "What is that thing out there?"

His coworker looked at the boat and said, "Those are Boom Boats! They are used to gather in the logs floating in the water. They are *incredibly* hard to drive!"

"What makes them so hard to drive?" my uncle asked curiously.

"They don't have a steering wheel. The boat needs to be able to go in any direction so instead of a steering wheel there is a stick in the middle of the boat that is used for steering." He continued, "It takes guys *years* to be good at driving them so there aren't many guys who can."

My uncle's curiosity was officially piqued! He *needed* to get into one of those boats.

During lunch the next day, he asked the foreman if he could give it a try.

The foreman looked at him and said, "Do you know how to drive it?"

"No," my uncle said, "But I'm sure I can figure it out."

"Haha…it's very difficult, but go ahead, give it a shot," his boss said chuckling, "We need some lunch time entertainment anyways!"

Over the next few months, my uncle used all of his breaks to learn to drive the Boom Boat. His coworkers couldn't figure out why he was spending all his break time on driving this crazy little boat. Till one day when one of the Boom Boat drivers was not able to come to work.

The supervisor called a meeting.

"Chris is sick and can't drive today, and Henry our back-up driver is on holidays. Gentlemen, we *need* someone to drive this thing?! Can any of you drive the Boom Boat?"

It was like a heavenly choir was singing in my uncle's ears. The moment that he had been *preparing* for had arrived!

"Sir, I do," my uncle said with his hand up.

"Wayne? You? When did you learn how to operate one of those?!" the Supervisor asked.

"Well Sir, I have been using all my breaks for the past few months to practice driving them," my uncle continued, "I knew that there were no positions available to be a Boom Boat driver but I figured that if I learned how to drive them, then maybe one day an opportunity would come to drive."

The Supervisor looked at my uncle, smiled and said, "Your day is here! Get out there!"

We never know if and when our opportunity will come.

Are you willing to prepare for an opportunity that may possibly NEVER happen?

We can't control WHEN or IF the opportunities come our way, but we can prepare ourselves to take advantage of the opportunities if they do come.

Being mission driven will keep you from *waiting* on opportunities and propel you to *prepare* for them each day.

TRAIN TO BE CLUTCH

- What are you doing to prepare for your opportunity of your dreams?

CHAPTER 75

THE MOST CRUCIAL COMPONENT OF A GROWTH MINDSET

WE WERE SITTING with some young women who happened to be world class at hitting a little white ball around a field, and Jamie said something that blew my mind!

"You have to have a growth mindset about having a growth mindset"

Simple.

Profound.

MASSIVE implications!

If you are anything like me, you catch yourself, quite often in my case, slipping back into old habits of operating from a fixed mindset.

So, when Jamie said that statement I literally felt a weight lift off my shoulders.

Yes! That's it! Beating myself up over falling back into the fixed mindset is counter productive.

This is a journey, it's not a test. It is going to take time and patience to develop a growth mindset in all areas of our life.

The key is to remember to have a growth mindset about having a growth mindset.

"The key to success is to keep growing as a team."
— Phil Jackson, *Eleven Rings: The Soul of Success*

TRAIN TO BE CLUTCH

- Watch the YouTube video "Carol Dweck- A Study On Praise And Mindsets"
- Write out your What Went Well Journal

CHAPTER 76

PUT A NUMBER ON IT

"Work harder!!!"

"SPRINT!!!"

"The effort wasn't good enough today."

"No one was focused today."

"Your attitude sucks today."

These are common phrases you hear all over the country from people in leadership positions. However, they are really ambiguous and don't *actually* communicate much other than the leader's frustration.

Rather than yelling out these ambiguous phrases, what if we started to put a number on it?

For example:

"I think your effort right now is a 4, and your attitude is a 7. How about for the next 10 minutes we try and get our effort to a 7 and our attitude to a 9?"

"YES! Joshua, *THAT* sprint was a 10! I want you to do your best to get to *THAT* level of effort every time."

"Jessica, I think your attitude has been at an 8 or higher this month, but your work ethic and focus have been around a 5. We value you as a member of this team, and in order to continue being on the team we are going to have to see you get your work ethic and focus up closer to an 8."

Now, I will be the first to say these are still arbitrary numbers and completely relative. However, when we put a number on it, it just helps us to have a better understanding of what the person leading is seeing in us and what they are looking for in the future.

Often times we are asking new people to do things they have never done before. In Greek they differentiate between having head knowledge of something and experiential knowledge of something.

Eidein is used to describe the head knowledge, where as the word *gnsosis* is used to describe a more intimate and personal understanding through experience.

When we are trying to help those we lead tap into areas of perseverance, growth, and ability they never knew they had inside of them, it is helpful to make things as tangible as possible.

"Look, I understand you *feel* like you are working harder than you have ever worked in your life, and you probably *are* working harder than you have ever worked. BUT the old standard you were used to was actually a 4 in terms of your *true* potential. Do you want to tap into your greatest potential, or do you want to settle for what was good enough at a much lower level?"

TRAIN TO BE CLUTCH

- What are 2 areas where your communication could benefit from putting a number on it?

CHAPTER 77

POWER QUESTIONS

"I'LL BE HONEST with you, you absolutely crushed that kid with your questions."

"I know," she said. "I feel so bad, but what else could I have asked him?"

I had been training this lady for a few months at this point and she was working at some junior golf events in her hometown. One day as she saw 2 young kids coming in from their round she asked them 2 of the laziest questions we can ask.

"What'd you shoot?" she asked. One guy started smiling as he told her that he shot one under. The other guy just lowered his head and shamefully said he shot in the 90's.

Feeling bad, she followed up with, "Well, did you have fun?"

It may not seem like it, but our questions really show what we value. When you came home from a game or round when you were younger, what was one of the first questions someone who wasn't there would ask?

"Did you win?"
"What did you shoot?"
"How many minutes did you play?"
"How many points did you score?"

"One thing I've learned as a coach is that you can't force your will on people. If you want them to act differently, you need to inspire them to change themselves."
— Phil Jackson, *Eleven Rings: The Soul of Success*

TRAIN TO BE CLUTCH

- Write down 2 specific questions that you will ask your teammates, kids, or colleagues today. Don't elaborate. Don't teach. Just ask and listen.
- Read: *Power Questions* by Andrew Sobel

CHAPTER 78

MOVING FROM *WHAT IF* TO EVEN IF

I WONDER WHAT would happen if we changed our "*what if* this seemingly bad thing happens" to "*even if* this seemingly bad thing happens."

As I was writing this chapter I was standing in a line behind at least 3,000 people waiting for a chance to buy the new iPhone 6 plus. None of us knew if they were going to have enough in stock for all of us, and it was easy to let my focus go to "what if I woke up at 4:52am to stand in line for 5 hours and NOT get a phone?!"

This type of rumination is not very helpful for peace and tranquility. It can lead to anxiety and frustration.

Here are some other examples:

- What if I treat my team with love and respect and we don't win?!
- What if I fight for my marriage for 2 years and my spouse still chooses to leave me?
- What if I give my very very best, make tons of sacrifices, and I don't make it to the league?
- What if I put people over profit and our business fails?
- What if I believe and pray for my son to be healed and he still dies at the age of 7?

Scary thoughts.

We can't control outcomes, but we do have control over a few things, and it usually works out best when we use our energy on those things.

So, I wonder what would happen if we changed our "what if's" to "even if's."

- Even if I do not get a new iPhone today, I will have an opportunity to develop more patience.
- Even if I do not make it to the league, I will know I gave it my all and will have developed characteristics that will help me in other facets of life.
- Even if my spouse chooses to leave me, I will know I did everything I could to save our marriage.
- Even if our business fails, we will have learned a lot of valuable lessons for the future.
- Even if my son dies, I will continue to trust in Jesus and believe God is good.

We don't know what you are facing or have just been through. But we have been through our share of tragedy, loss, and pain. We don't have control over what happens most of the time. However, we do have control over whether or not we ruminate on negative outcomes or we choose to look at them as, "*Even if* this happens I will not quit, I will not give in, I will persevere, I will trust, I will live a courageous life."

> "Everything can be taken from a man but one thing: the last of the human freedoms—to choose one's attitude in any given set of circumstances, to choose one's own way."
> Viktor Frankl –Holocaust Survivor and Author of, *Man's Search For Meaning.*

CHAPTER 79

PEACE AND JOY UNDER PRESSURE

How CAN YOU have hope, joy, and a clear head in the midst of incredible pressure?

> Pressure tends to cause people to make poor decisions.
> Pressure does weird things to people.
> People do stupid things under pressure.

The night before Jesus was sold out by one of His disciples and abandoned by the rest of them, He wanted out of the cross. He asked God 3 different times to "let this cup pass from me."

> How did He make it through this situation in spite of His feelings?

> He leaned into His "Abba" Father. In Hebrew Abba is what a very young hild would call their father. Similar to "Da-da" or even like a baby only able to say "Da."

> When the pressure rises, when the storms come, and they always will, we can lean into our "Abba" Father and His love.

> Love kept Jesus on His mission. The *perfect* love of our Father.

> *Everything comes down to this: can we believe we are the object of God's unconditional, undeserved, passionate, relentless, and steadfast love?*

Remember, the Holy Spirit, which is inside of us when we entrust our life to Jesus, is the great encourager.

The Devil is the great accuser.

Don't trust your feelings.
Trust in Jesus' finished work.
Trust in God's promises.

Feelings come and go.
His promises always come back true.
Don't trust your feelings.
Trust His promises.

Never will I leave you. Never will I forsake you. (*NIV* Hebrews 13:5)

The steadfast love of the Lord endures forever. (*ESV* Lamentations 3:22)

Perfect love casts out fear. (*ESV* 1 John 4:18)

Trust in the Lord with all your heart, lean not on your own understanding, in all your ways acknowledge Him, and He will direct your paths. (*NIV* Proverbs 3:5-6)

For God SO loved the world that He gave His one and only Son, that whoever believes in Him shall not perish, but have eternal life. (*NIV* John 3:16)

We are more than a conqueror through Him who loved us. (*NIV* Romans 8:37)

Come to Me (Jesus) all you who are weary and burdened and I will give you rest. (*NIV* Matthew 11:28)

He who began a good work in you will carry it on to completion. (*NIV* Philippians 1:16)

God is love. (*NIV* 1 John 4:8)

He gives power to the weak
and strength to the powerless.
Even youths will become weak and tired,
and young men will fall in exhaustion.
But those who trust in the Lord will find new strength.
They will soar high on wings like eagles.
They will run and not grow weary.
They will walk and not faint. (*New Living Translation*[8] Isaiah 40:29-31)

And I am convinced that nothing can ever separate us from God's love. Neither death nor life, neither angels nor demons, neither our fears for today nor our worries about tomorrow—not even the powers of hell can separate us from God's love. No power in the sky above or in the earth below—indeed, nothing in all creation will ever be able to separate us from the love of God that is revealed in Christ Jesus our Lord. (*NIV* Romans 8:38-39)

But all who listen to me will live in peace, untroubled by fear of harm. (*NLT* Proverbs 1:33)

I am leaving you with a gift—peace of mind and heart. And the peace I give is a gift the world cannot give. So don't be troubled or afraid. (*NLT* John 14:27)

---

8 *Holy Bible*, New Living Translation. Wheaton, Illinois; 1996, Tyndale House Publishers.

The thief cometh not, but for to steal, and to kill, and to destroy: I am come that they might have life, and that they might have it more abundantly. I am the good shepherd: the good shepherd giveth his life for the sheep. (*King James Version*[9] John 10:10-11)

*This chapter was written based off of my notes from a Judah Smith sermon in Los Angeles, California. To find out more you can go to his church website http://thecity.org or download the, *Jesus Is Music Project*, on iTunes or listen to it on YouTube.

TRAIN TO BE CLUTCH

- Think the life and resurrection of Jesus was a myth or just a cool story?
- Read the book: More *Than A Carpenter*
- Email: joshua@traintobeclutch.com for our comforting Bible verses mp3.

9 *The Holy Bible*, King James Version. New York: American Bible Society: 1999.

POSTSCRIPT

THE IMPETUS FOR this book came at the end of a three-hour conversation with a guy who coached one of the best teams in the country. He said to me, "I want the practical stuff."

The truth is that it's *not* practical.

It's often simple, but never easy.

There are things that are practical, but it is actually impractical to become a transformational leader.

It's like gardening.

You can cultivate a beautiful garden that is the very essence of life and beauty, but if you just let it be, the weeds will be back and take over in no time.

The journey to becoming a transformational leader is impractical, and it always will be. Transformational leadership is a life long journey of loving, serving, and putting first things first.

"If a team doesn't have the most essential ingredient—love—none of those other factors matter." –Phil Jackson

Tend your garden wisely with love.

CONTACT INFO:

Twitter: @joshuamedcalf | @jdgilbert19
Instagram: @realjoshuamedcalf | @jdgilbert19
Cell: *Joshua* 918-361-8611 | *Jamie* 918-884-9642
Email: Joshua@traintobeclutch.com & Jamie@traintobeclutch.com

Keynote Speaking- t2bc.com

Mentorship Program- Our mentorship program isn't a good fit for everyone, but we are always willing to see if it is a good fit for you. It is a serious investment of time and resources. Email Jamie@traintobeclutch.com for more information.

T2BC Reading Challenge- People are consistently telling us how going through our reading challenge has radically improved their business, family, and personal life. It is available to download under the *free stuff* tab at t2bc.com

The Experience- *Transformational Leadership Retreats.* We bring together people from all over the country to engage in a day of interactive learning. We also create space for fun activities like golf, surfing, or snowboarding with the t2bc team.

The Clutch Lab- Our T2BC podcast takes a deeper dive into leadership, life-skills, and mental training.

T2BC 101 Online Video Course- With over 20 short video sessions, you can use this course individually or to teach your team the T2BC curriculum. It is a great next step tool. Available at **t2bc.com/training**

Join the T2BC community- This is the best way for us to provide consistent value to your life and for us to develop a long term relationship. You will get articles, mp3's, videos, and other tools as they come out. It's also free. J Join at t2bc.com

Books- You can always order signed copies of any of our books by emailing us, and they are also available on iBooks, Kindle, Amazon, and through our publisher.

The first book we wrote is, ***Burn Your Goals***.
The second book we wrote is this one.
The third book Joshua wrote is, ***Hustle***
The fourth book Joshua wrote is, ***Chop Wood Carry Water***
The fifth book Jamie wrote is, ***The Principle Circle***
The sixth book Joshua wrote is, ***Pound The Stone.***

YouTube- Our channel is *train2bclutch*

THANK YOU'S FROM JAMIE

Yes, we have worked hard and try to be diligent with what we have. But none of this would be possible without God's steadfast love and faithfulness. There is no rational reason why I should have been born into the family I have, the country I live in, or with the capabilities and opportunities that I have. I have been near to death more times than I can count and I have done more than enough to disqualify myself from God's love. Nothing makes sense unless God is who he says He is. Thank you Father, for never changing.

I still believe that there are hundreds of thousands of people who have influenced my life and the way I think. So to everyone I've connected with, thank you.

More specifically, I want to thank my wife Amy. Thank you for loving Jesus more than you love me and for being my unconditional smile and support in everything. Now you are the peanut butter to my jelly!

To my son, James, your curiosity, fearlessness, and compassion for others challenges me more than you will ever know.

To my daughter, Ava, your faces drive me nuts.

To my parents, Karen and Lawrence, thank you for your unconditional love. I *still* cannot find one memory where you made me feel like my worth came from anything I did or did not do.

To Jim and Katie, thank you for allowing me to be a part of your family. You have loved me unconditionally and we thank you for your continual love and support in pursuit of our passions.

To Joshua, thank you for your unwavering love, dedication, and fearlessness as a leader. Moreover, thank you for being my best friend.

To all of the people in leadership whom I have had the pleasure to speak with and learn from, thank you!

THANK YOU'S FROM JOSHUA

To EVERYONE WHO has played a role in my life over the last 32 years, thank you!

I'm incredibly grateful to my mother who has supported me and been one of my best friends my whole life. Thank you for never giving up on me when no one would have blamed you if you had.

Thank you to my father who did the best he could with what he had.

Thank you to all the people who have given me the great privilege and responsibility of mentoring you. I have learned so much, and am truly grateful for that opportunity.

Thank you to Tim McClements for never giving up on me at Vanderbilt and helping me get a scholarship at Duke. I was a royal pain in your ass, and I'm forever grateful you stuck by my side.

I'm so grateful to Jamie and Amy, you both have been such an amazing support system in my life, and I'm so grateful I get to spend so much time with you. Thank you for creating a safe space for me to be me devoid of any judgment.

Thank you Amber for always listening to my stories. Hopefully one day you will learn something from them.

Thank you to Austin, TJ, Kyle, Joe, Pooter, Krause, Brady, Tim, and my many other friends who have been there for me during the many low points in my life.

Thank you Anson for all your words of encouragement and allowing me to work with your program.

Thank you Steph for being an amazing woman full of love, empathy, and creativity. Your childlike spirit encourages and inspires me every day. Your sunshine lights up the world ☺

Thank you Judah Smith for being the most amazing pastor a person could ask for. You have taught me so much about Jesus, how He really feels about me, and how I can live like Him. I don't think anyone has ever had such a profound impact on my life in such a short period of time as you have.

Thank you Lisa for always being there to hear my articles, or just to listen to another one of my crazy stories.

Thank you Cori for taking a chance on me and giving me the opportunity to work with your amazing program.

Thank you Russ and Skip for all the mentorship over the years. Thank you Skip for being one of the first people outside of my family to financially invest in me and my dreams.

Thank you Andy and Terry for teaching me so much as a teenager. I wouldn't be here today without your love and wisdom.

Thank you Adri for all your prayers and friendship.

Thank you Jesus for your extravagant and undeserved love.